THE RIVER COTTAGE YEAR

Hugh Fearnley-Whittingstall

Photography by Simon Wheeler

www.rivercottage.net

Hodder & Stoughton

Text © 2003 Hugh Fearnley-Whittingstall
Photography © 2003 Simon Wheeler
First published in Great Britain in 2003 by Hodder and Stoughton
A division of Hodder Headline

10 9 8 7

A CIP catalogue record for this title is available from the British Library

ISBN 0 340 82821 8

Design by Georgia Vaux

Typeset in Perpetua and Advert Rough

Printed and bound in Great Britain by Butler & Tanner

Hodder and Stoughton
A division of Hodder Headline
338 Euston Road
London NW1 3BH

For Andrew and Zam, with love and thanks

HUGH'S ACKNOWLEDGEMENTS

This book is the product of a brilliant team with whom I have hugely enjoyed working. Let's do some more. Massive thanks to you all, especially to Simon Wheeler, for stunning photography that always finds a new angle; to Richard Atkinson, for admirably high standards enforced with maximum charm, minimum fuss; to Georgia Vaux, for a simply brilliant design, and lots of tea; to Bryan Johnson, for essential help and a sure touch in the kitchen; to Jane Middleton, for superb copy-editing and sensitive recipe-testing; to my agent Antony Topping, for sanely handling a crazy year. Thanks also to the entire team at Hodder, including (but by no means limited to!) Jo Seaton, Kerry Hood, Leigh Goodman, Alasdair Oliver and Briar Silich. Thanks to all who contributed to the success of River Cottage, the television series, especially Ben Frow, Nick Powell, Richard Ellingham and everyone at KEO Films. Thanks to Rob Love for the exciting possibilities that are rivercottage.net. Thanks to Bernie James and Frank and Nicola Greenway for help with the livestock, and Steve and Dide Lucas for help with the garden. Many thanks and much love, as always, to Marie and Oscar — not least for eating it all up.

BEAMINSTER SUMMER SHOW

SATURDAY AUGUST 17th 19** 2002

COND PRIZE

A JAR OF CHUTNEY

TOR H WHITTINGTON

CONTENTS

Why cook seasonally? _ _ _ _ _ _ _ _ _ _ _ _ _ _ _ _

This is a book about seasonal cookery. I've written it because I believe passionately that those who shop and cook in harmony with the seasons will get immeasurably more pleasure and satisfaction from their food than those who don't. I've also written it because I've observed, with mounting alarm, that our sense of seasonality is under threat.

The supermarkets must take the lion's share of the blame. For the most part, they seem not merely uninterested in seasonality but often keen to suppress it. They source produce throughout the world that homogenises their product range into a year-long display of cosy familiarity. Of necessity, the seasons still exert some influence on their stocking policy. Yet they will do everything possible to disguise this fact when presenting produce to their customers. They fear that seasonally driven marketing will result in inconsistent spending. They don't want to encourage their customers to think seasonally, because they believe seasonality is not profitable.

It is a policy that is damaging the soul of British cooking. But I believe that it's a policy that is also misconceived. It rests on an assumption that the British food shopper is fundamentally lazy, unresponsive to the concept of seasonal inspiration, and more interested in maintaining old and regular habits than exploring new and exciting possibilities.

This is, of course, a circular and self-fulfilling strategy. Deny consumers the chance to show an independent spirit and guess what? Amazingly, they fail to show much of an independent spirit. This can hardly be good for business.

The downside of the culture of infinite year-round choice is a kind of options paralysis, or consumer lethargy: there's so much on offer that you don't know where to start. Surely an understanding of the seasons would help free shoppers from this ball and chain. Why not make British produce in season – which is when it is at its best – the heart and soul of the store (if supermarkets can be said to possess either of these attributes)? The supermarket that dares to be different in this respect might just pull ahead of its dull and indistinguishable rivals.

Until this happens, if it ever does, supermarket shoppers will have to make a conscious effort to find the best fresh, local and seasonal produce hidden away among the jet-lagged imports. Fortunately, the fact that supermarkets are usually decent enough to label fruit and veg with their country of origin means this is not an entirely hopeless task. But the alternative I would recommend is to seek out a genuinely local greengrocer's, farm shop or farmers' market, or a local box delivery scheme, where the produce is almost by definition both seasonal and locally grown. My website, www.rivercottage.net, will help you explore these options.

In the four years I spent at River Cottage, and at the farm nearby where I now live, my own sense of the British seasons has flourished. They will, if we let them, feed us fabulously well. I have not the least doubt that I am a better cook and a happier person for having absorbed the rhythms of the growing year. I love the sense of anticipation and seizing the moment that goes with getting to know the shifting seasons: in the garden, on the farm, in the hedgerow and even down on the coast.

Of course, if you grow and gather your own food you can hardly fail to appreciate the seasons and their impact on the kitchen. So what about those who don't? The majority who buy all, and grow none, of their food. In an age where the transport of food between the hemispheres is increasingly fast and furious, the question inevitably arises, why bother with seasonality? Maybe the supermarkets have got it right. Why not simply embrace the extraordinary array of choice we now have and cook what we want, when we want?

This is a big and important question. And I am aware that not all supposed food-lovers agree with me about the answer. Much of the way cookery is presented in Britain – in books, colour supplements and on television – works against our understanding and appreciation of the seasons. It does so by fostering a 'grass is greener' mentality, making us aspire to someone else's seasonality (or, ironically, their relative lack of it). It implies that the food and produce of sunnier climes (the Mediterranean in particular) are more worthwhile than our own. In short, it idolises the exotic.

To those who perpetrate this idea, it may be a genuine source of regret that we do not have an endless summer in this country. I feel no such pangs. On the contrary, I think we have one of the richest experiences of the seasons of any country on earth. And we have a range of produce and a culinary heritage that reflect that experience and help to make us who we are. Our weather may be the butt of longstanding jokes among our Continental neighbours, and consequently, in that self-effacing British way, among ourselves. But don't we love it really? Isn't our summer so special precisely because, just like our autumn, our winter and our spring, it doesn't last forever?

This sense of identity with our climate and the landscape it creates may not matter to everyone. But there are more practical and universal reasons for shopping seasonally. For example, what is locally seasonal will, with negligible exceptions, be far better than what is not. Most fresh produce doesn't travel well, and the various processes and technologies applied to help it travel better are invariably detrimental to its eating qualities. By contrast, seasonal produce, locally grown, can be harvested and eaten at its best.

Seasonality leads us not just to fresher, less travel-weary produce but also to better-tasting varieties of our home-grown favourites. Despite the overwhelming trend of globalisation and industrialisation of food, there are still small producers in this country dedicated to the art of cultivating the best varieties of our seasonal produce – fruit and vegetables that have not been genetically improved for the sake of shelf life, nor inoculated for long-distance travel. Such committed individuals are the guardians of the vital variations in the taste and texture of produce that allow us, by turns, to be individuals in our own taste – our safeguard against a future of bland homogeneity. If we do not use them, we will lose them.

Finally, the fact that local, seasonal produce comes without a punitive cost to the environment, in terms of fossil fuels burnt in transportation, is a bonus many will appreciate.

I don't want to get too po-faced and ascetic about this, wagging a disapproving finger at those who are tempted by a Costa Rican pineapple in July or Moroccan clementines at Christmas. For a start, you're going to be waiting a long time before those English pineapples finally come into season! And I would be a hypocrite and a liar if I said I denied myself the undoubted pleasures of such exotics. Bananas, for example, are a daily staple in our house, as in millions of others.

The simple fact is we can't grow bananas, pineapples and clementines in this country. And I have no wish to deny other agricultural communities the chance to sell their delightful produce in the global marketplace. I simply believe that an engagement with the global should be secondary to an engagement with the local. What is local and seasonal should be at the forefront of each shopper's consciousness – and indeed of his or her conscience. (Incidentally, the scandalous politics and protectionism of the banana trade are a can of worms I would gladly open elsewhere. For now I'll just declare my preference for the Fairtrade banana, which, happily, is increasingly available in this country.)

Nor do I wish to be over-prescriptive about the parameters of seasonal eating. The seasons cannot be rigidly defined. They are fluid and unpredictable. You can't make a date in your diary for the first strawberry or the last Brussels sprout, any more than you can for the first cuckoo or the last departing swallow. They'll do what they have to do, and they'll do it in their own time.

I'd like you to apply a similar easy latitude to the way you use and interpret this book. I chose the twelve months rather than the four seasons as an organising principle because I wanted to present, both visually and in the recipes, the sense of a slowly evolving year rather than four distinct seasonal ghettos. I actually want you to blur the edges between the chapters in your mind. And I'd be happy for you to conclude that most of the recipes in this book can probably be enjoyed in the month either side of the one in which they appear.

This is particularly true of the winter months, where we see a slowing down of the whole seasonal dynamo. A kind of stasis is reached in the produce available. I'd even go so far as to say that you could swap my January recipes for my February ones and still be true to the seasons. My selection is based less on availability than on the idea that even greater comfort is called for in February, as our patience with winter begins to wear thin. Though whether my rice pudding is more comforting than my roly-poly could be a matter for lively debate.

In describing and illustrating the seasonal rhythms of our growing and cooking year here in Dorset, I hope I will inspire some more of you to grow your own food. Far more importantly, I hope I will inspire *all* of you to put British seasonal produce at the very heart of your cooking. Because, in the end, seasonal cooking is not a high-minded duty or a restrictive chore but a liberating pleasure. In a world where our approach to food often seems a kind of madness, seasonality is sanity. It offers the best and quickest solution to the never-ending question, what shall I cook today?

A guide to seasonal British produce

I would love everyone to grow at least some of their own food, but I know that's wishful thinking. However, I really don't see why it should be an unrealistic aim to persuade everyone who is remotely interested in good food to make seasonal British produce the number-one priority on their shopping list. After all it will, almost without exception, be the best food available on the day.

The four lists below are intended as quick reference guides – not only to the best of British fruit and vegetables but also to the wild food larder, and to items of fish, shellfish and game whose quality or availability varies significantly with the seasons.

A pale green blob-in-the-box indicates seasonal availability of British specimens in the month in question, while a dark green blob indicates when you may expect an item to be at its absolute best. (You'll see, for example, that there's really very little reason, at any time of year, to buy cabbages or carrots that are not UK-produced.)

I'm not going to get too preachy about organic produce here. I garden and farm organically and I believe passionately that this is the best thing for the health of our land. But flying organic produce halfway round the world in fuel-guzzling planes makes something of a mockery of the supermarkets' 'more environmental than thou' sentiments. So I would put local and seasonal a rung above organic as a priority. And I would highly recommend farmers' markets, farm shops and box delivery schemes as the best places to source such produce. If the produce is organic too, then so much the better.

Just one more thought – if it isn't too patronising: cast your eyes quickly down the lists below and ask yourself how many of the items listed you have actually tasted, ideally British grown, in the last twelve months. If the answer isn't 'all of them', then ask yourself why not? And see if you can make that the answer one year from now.

Note

Like daylight hours and average temperature, the prime seasonality of cultivated fruit and vegetables, and of hedgerow plants, varies from the south to the north of the country. I must confess that the charts below are based on the southerner's calendar – in particular on the reliably mild climate of Dorset. Both the onset of availability and the prime season for much of the produce in the tables may therefore be as much as three or four weeks later in the north.

A – Z of vegetables in season

It is perhaps vegetables more than any other produce that define the cook's sense of the season. Spring greens, summer peas and beans, autumn squashes and winter roots – even if you have just that basic sense of what is best when, then you already have something precious.

But I'm urging you to go further. Because I know that developing your seasonal familiarity with the vegetables that we grow to such a superbly high standard in this country is one of the biggest favours you can do yourself as a cook.

For it is vegetables, not fish or meat, that are the cook's greatest asset, and the building blocks of the best meals. I explored this theme in some detail in the garden section of *The River Cottage Cookbook* but you have only to look at the list below and it becomes almost self-evident. Just consider the vast array of textures and flavours on offer. Then imagine the different effects that can be achieved with different cooking techniques: boiling, mashing, roasting, grilling, frying. Start combining them with each other, then with fish and meat.

This is at least as true for those who shop for vegetables as for those who grow their own. The shopper may not always be spoilt for choice. The search is for what is best and freshest on the day. If you are shopping in the right place, that is almost certain to be something local and in season.

Become a hunter-gatherer vegetable shopper, with a scrupulous eye for quality. Soon you will almost instinctively anticipate the seasonal arrival of the items below with a sensual relish.

○ = in season   ● = at its best

	jan	feb	mar	apr	may	jun	jul	aug	sep	oct	nov	dec
ARTICHOKES (Jerusalem)	●	●	○							○	●	●
ARTICHOKES (globe)				○	○	●	●	●	○			
ASPARAGUS				○	●	●						
AUBERGINES						○	●	●	○			
BEETROOT	○	○				○	●	●	●	●	●	○
BORLOTTI BEANS (for podding)							○	●	●	○		
BROAD BEANS					○	●	●	●	○			
BROCCOLI (purple sprouting)	○	○	●	●	○							○
BROCCOLI (calabrese)						○	○	●	●	●	○	
BRUSSELS SPROUTS	●	●	○							○	○	●
BRUSSELS TOPS	●	●									●	●
CABBAGES (various green varieties)	●	●	●	●	●	○	○	●	●	●	●	●
CABBAGES (white)	●	●	○							○	●	●

	jan	feb	mar	apr	may	jun	jul	aug	sep	oct	nov	dec
CABBAGES (red)	●	●							●	●	●	●
CARDOONS									●	●	●	●
CARROTS	●	●	●	●	●	●	●	●	●	●	●	●
CAULIFLOWER			●	●	●	●	●	●	●	●	●	●
CELERIAC	●	●	●							●	●	●
CELERY	●	●							●	●	●	●
CHARD	●	●	●	●	●		●	●		●	●	●
CHICORY	●	●	●	●					●	●	●	●
COURGETTES							●	●	●	●		
CUCUMBER						●	●	●	●	●		
ENDIVE	●	●	●	●					●	●	●	●
FENNEL							●	●	●	●		
FRENCH BEANS (whole pod)							●	●	●	●		
GARLIC						●	●	●	●	●		
GREENS (spring & winter)	●	●	●	●	●						●	●
KALE (& borecole)	●	●	●	●					●	●	●	●
KOHLRABI	●	●					●	●	●	●	●	●
LAMB'S LETTUCE					●	●	●	●	●	●	●	
LEEKS	●	●	●	●					●	●	●	●
LETTUCE	●	●	●	●	●	●	●	●	●	●	●	●
ONIONS	●	●	●	●	●	●	●	●	●	●	●	●
PAK CHOI	●	●				●	●	●	●	●	●	●
PARSNIPS	●	●	●						●	●	●	●
PEAS, INCLUDING SUGAR SNAPS						●	●	●	●	●		
PEPPERS AND CHILLIES								●	●	●	●	
POTATOES	●	●	●	●	●	●	●	●	●	●	●	●
PUMPKINS (& squashes)								●	●	●	●	●
PURSLANE						●	●	●	●	●		
RADISHES	●	●		●	●	●	●	●	●	●	●	●
ROCKET	●	●	●	●	●	●	●	●	●	●	●	●
RUNNER BEANS								●	●	●		
SALSIFY (& scorzonera)	●	●						●	●	●	●	●
SAMPHIRE								●	●			
SEA KALE			●	●	●							
SORREL		●	●	●	●	●	●	●	●	●	●	●
SPINACH	●	●	●	●	●	●		●	●	●	●	●
SWEDE	●	●	●						●	●	●	●
SWEETCORN								●	●	●	●	●
TOMATOES							●	●	●	●	●	
TURNIPS	●	●						●	●	●	●	●
WATERCRESS	●	●	●	●	●	●	●	●	●	●	●	●

A – Z of fruit in season

My primary aim in this book is to celebrate the diversity of seasonal British produce – and to urge you to do likewise. But I am not such a spoilsport as to insist that you overlook the best of the seasonal fruit crop from the Continent, at least where fruits that we will always struggle to produce ourselves are concerned. British cherries and greengages are (sadly) a rarity. Peaches and apricots will grow here, but only if lovingly attended by obsessives. You may be lucky enough to know one. Otherwise, like the rest of us, you will be in the market for Continental imports. They have their moments, too, and it is as well to know when you can taste them at their best.

So, along with the British fruits, I include in the table below a few honorary mentions of the pick of the Continental crop. The tropical exotics, such as citrus, bananas, mangoes etc, I'll pass on here – not that I'm such an ascetic as to shun them altogether. But the food miles do make me wince, so I try to redress the balance by buying Fairtrade where possible.

As to varieties of our abundant apples and pears, it would be pointless to attempt an exhaustive list, so I have simply suggested some personal favourites across the seasons.

I think it is worth noting just how short the time frame for some of our native fruits can be. Take your eye off the ball and suddenly they're over. I say, fill your boots while you can.

	jan	feb	mar	apr	may	jun	jul	aug	sep	oct	nov	dec
APPLES (early) (Discovery, George Cave, Redsleeves)								●	●			
APPLES (late) (Egremont Russet, Blenheim Orange, Orleans Reinette)									●	●	●	●
APPLES (store) (Cox's, Fiesta, Ashmead's Kernel, Bramley)	●	●	●							●	●	●
APRICOTS (fresh, imported)					●	●	●	●				
BLACKBERRIES (cultivated)							●	●	●	●		
BLACKCURRANTS						●	●	●	●			
BLUEBERRIES							●	●	●			
CHERRIES (European)						●	●	●	●			
CHERRIES (home grown)						●	●	●				
DAMSONS									●	●		
GOOSEBERRIES						●	●	●				
GRAPES (English hothouse)										●		
GREENGAGES							●	●	●			
LOGANBERRIES							●	●	●			
MEDLARS											●	●

	jan	feb	mar	apr	may	jun	jul	aug	sep	oct	nov	dec
MELONS (imported Charentais)							●	●	●	●		
PEACHES & NECTARINES (imported)							●	●	●	●		
PEARS (early–mid) (Beth, Williams, Merton Pride)								●	●	●		
PEARS (late) (Concorde, Doyenne du Comice, Conference, Winter Nellis)	●									●	●	●
PLUMS								●	●			
QUINCE										●	●	●
RASPBERRIES							●	●	●	●	●	
REDCURRANTS							●	●	●			
RHUBARB (forced)	●	●	●	●								●
RHUBARB (outdoor)				●	●	●	●	●	●	●		
STRAWBERRIES							●	●	●	●		
WHITE CURRANTS							●	●				
WORCESTERBERRIES							●	●	●	●		

A – Z of fish, shellfish and game in season

It is not just plants that are subject to seasonal variations. The seasons also affect the suitability for the pot of our edible animals: fish, shellfish, birds and mammals.

There are two aspects to this. First, a 'natural' season, when we can predict that certain species are likely to be in their prime, owing to abundant feeding and/or a natural growth cycle. Second, an imposed 'closed' season, when we decide that we will not kill or harvest the creature in question during its breeding season, as a measure to prevent decline in numbers. Both these seasonal effects are taken into account in the table below.

Having said that, the seasonal behaviour and condition of things with legs, wings, scales and shells are intrinsically a little harder to predict than those of plants. Springs can be early or late, winters harsh or mild, and animals are fast to respond to such fluctuations.

On our coastal waters such natural variations have been further exaggerated by the undeniable effects of climate change. Mackerel and sea bass are increasingly found inshore in the winter and spring, as well as the summer and autumn months. Oysters may go 'milky' at odd times of the year. And creatures such as triggerfish and octopus that were once occasional visitors seem to be looking for residential status. So the list below is, of necessity, approximate. If you should find a specimen conspicuously 'out of season', then congratulations – you must be thinking seasonally already.

	jan	feb	mar	apr	may	jun	jul	aug	sep	oct	nov	dec
Fish												
BLACK BREAM					•	•	•	•	•	•	•	•
COD	•	•	•	•	•	•	•	•	•	•	•	•
CRAYFISH, SIGNAL (freshwater)				•	•	•	•	•	•			
EELS				•	•	•	•	•	•	•		
MACKEREL	•	•	•	•	•	•	•	•	•	•	•	•
POLLACK	•	•	•	•	•	•	•	•	•	•	•	•
SALMON (wild)	•	•	•	•	•	•	•	•	•			
SEA BASS	•	•	•	•	•	•	•	•	•	•	•	•
SEA TROUT			•	•	•	•	•	•	•			
SPRATS	•								•	•	•	•
TROUT, RIVER (i.e. brown & rainbow)				•	•	•	•	•	•	•		
WHITING	•	•								•	•	•
Shellfish												
COCKLES	•	•	•	•	•	•	•	•	•	•	•	•
CRAB (brown, cock)	•	•	•	•	•	•	•	•	•	•	•	•
CRAB (brown, hen)	•	•	•	•	•	•	•	•	•	•	•	•
CRAB (spider)	•	•	•	•	•	•	•	•	•	•	•	•
CUTTLEFISH				•	•	•	•	•				
LOBSTER	•	•	•	•	•	•	•	•	•	•	•	•
MUSSELS	•	•	•	•	•	•	•	•	•	•	•	•
OYSTERS (native)	•	•	•	•					•	•	•	•
OYSTERS (rock)	•	•	•	•	•	•	•	•	•	•	•	•
PRAWNS						•	•	•	•	•	•	•
SCALLOPS	•	•	•	•	•	•	•	•	•	•	•	•
SQUID	•								•	•	•	•
Game												
GOOSE (wild)	•									•	•	•
GOOSE (farmed)	•								•	•	•	•
GREY SQUIRREL	•	•	•	•	•	•	•	•	•	•	•	•
GROUSE	•							•	•	•	•	•
HARE	•	•	•							•	•	•
MALLARD	•	•							•	•	•	•
PARTRIDGE	•	•							•	•	•	•
PHEASANT	•	•								•	•	•
RABBIT	•	•	•	•	•	•	•	•	•	•	•	•
SNIPE	•									•	•	•
WOODCOCK	•									•	•	•
WOOD PIGEON	•	•	•	•	•	•	•	•	•	•	•	•
	jan	feb	mar	apr	may	jun	jul	aug	sep	oct	nov	dec

A – Z of popular edible wild plants in season

By definition, the items on this list are likely to be rather more elusive than cultivated fruit and vegetables. But at the right time and in the right place, they can all be abundant – and delicious. And it's surprising what a rich haul can often be had at the margins of even a small garden.

Perhaps the first pattern to note from the list below is the distinctive seasonal surge of the wild 'leafy greens', compared to their cultivated cousins. Such useful plants as chickweed, hogweed, fat hen, nettles, wild garlic and watercress are often peeping through as early as February – and are usually quite pickable by March. At the other end of the year, the hedgerow conveniently holds back its fruit harvest until most of the cultivated soft fruits have finished. Bilberries and blackberries will keep you in fruit for September, while sloes, rowans and crab apples add interest to October.

Once you've got the hang of the basic rhythms of this list, then a walk in the country at any time of year is certain to have food-gathering potential.

Greens

	jan	feb	mar	apr	may	jun	jul	aug	sep	oct	nov	dec
ALEXANDERS			●	●	●							
BROOM BUDS				●	●	●						
CHICKWEED		●	●	●	●	●	●	●	●	●		
DANDELIONS			●	●	●							
FAT HEN			●	●	●	●	●	●	●			
HOGWEED SHOOTS			●	●	●	●						
HOP SHOOTS				●	●							
MARSH SAMPHIRE						●	●	●	●			
NETTLES	●	●	●	●	●	●	●	●	●	●	●	●
SEA KALE			●	●								
SEA SPINACH			●	●	●	●	●	●	●	●	●	●
SORREL		●	●	●	●	●	●	●	●	●		
WATERCRESS			●	●	●	●	●	●	●	●	●	
WILD ROCKET (leaves)			●	●	●	●	●	●				

Herbs

	jan	feb	mar	apr	may	jun	jul	aug	sep	oct	nov	dec
CHIVES		●	●	●	●	●	●	●	●	●	●	
COW PARSLEY (aka wild chervil)	●	●	●	●						●	●	●
HORSERADISH					●	●	●	●	●	●		
MEADOWSWEET (leaves)			●	●	●							
WILD FENNEL				●	●	●	●	●	●	●		
WILD GARLIC			●	●	●							

	jan	feb	mar	apr	may	jun	jul	aug	sep	oct	nov	dec
Flowers												
ELDERFLOWERS					●	●	●					
PRIMROSES (garden)		●	●	●	●							
Fruits												
BILBERRIES (aka blaeberries)							●	●	●			
BLACKBERRIES							●	●	●	●		
BULLACE								●	●	●		
CRAB APPLES									●	●	●	●
ELDERBERRIES									●	●		
JUNIPER BERRIES	●	●						●	●	●	●	●
ROSEHIPS										●	●	●
ROWAN BERRIES									●	●	●	
SLOES									●	●	●	
WILD STRAWBERRIES						●	●	●	●			
Fungi												
CEPS (aka porcini)							●	●	●	●	●	
CHANTERELLES						●	●	●	●	●	●	
CHICKEN OF THE WOODS						●	●	●	●	●	●	
FIELD MUSHROOMS							●	●	●	●		
HEDGEHOG FUNGUS								●	●	●	●	●
HORSE MUSHROOMS							●	●	●	●	●	●
MORELS			●	●	●	●						
OYSTER MUSHROOMS (pleurottes)				●	●	●	●	●	●	●	●	●
PARASOL MUSHROOMS							●	●	●	●	●	●
PUFFBALLS, GIANT							●	●	●	●		
ST GEORGE'S MUSHROOMS				●	●	●						
SHAGGY INK CAPS									●	●	●	
SUMMER TRUFFLES							●	●	●	●	●	
WOOD BLEWITS									●	●	●	●
Nuts												
CHESTNUTS	●	●							●	●	●	●
HAZELNUTS								●	●			
PIGNUTS					●	●	●	●				
WALNUTS									●	●	●	
Saps (!)												
BIRCH SAP			●	●								

JANUARY _____

January's okay. I like it, in fact. It's the proper winter month, without December's distracting festivities and February's battle against gloom and despondency (see next chapter!). And my birthday, an occasion I always like to mark in the kitchen, falls slap in the middle of the month. The tipsy fruity roly-poly (page 38) makes a wonderful winter birthday cake.

With Christmas out of the way, this is the month to ask yourself what really thrills you from the winter repertoire, and to set about cooking it with great gusto. Have you had enough game this season? See if you can track down a mallard, a teal, a brace of woodcock, or two of snipe. And when did you last treat yourself to one of those classic carnivorous comfort dishes with bones to gnaw at, such as oxtail stew, braised lamb shanks or shin of beef (page 30)? Are you a secret sprout-lover, vetoed by the rest of the family from wheeling out the little brassica buds at Christmas? Now's the time to indulge your passion . . .

In fact, it's a good time to make creative space for any number of undervalued winter vegetables, and perhaps give them an outing on their own for a change rather than just serve them plain boiled and 'on the side'.

Think particularly of the winter roots – not just carrots and potatoes but what I call the 'aromatic roots': celeriac, Jerusalem artichokes, parsnips, salsify and scorzonera. They all make wonderful rich, creamy purées, both on their own and combined with each other in mathematically limitless ratios. And they can be served at almost any consistency, from a coarse, chunky mash to a velvety smooth soup (see pages 35–7 for various suggestions, and go from there). They can also all be used to make a winter warmer whose creamy interior and crusty top never fail to charm those who eat it – the gratin. If, by chance, you have never eaten a salsify gratin, and especially if you've never tried salsify at all, you are in for a stunning new taste experience (page 37).

You can, if you like, safely ignore the outdoor garden for the entire month, except to gather your winter greens and any of the above-mentioned roots you have taken the trouble to cultivate. Or you can, if you prefer, be a busy garden bee – frost permitting. There's no point in breaking your spade on earth as hard as concrete, but a spell of mild weather will allow you to do a spot of digging, or plant the fruit trees and bushes you didn't get round to planting before Christmas.

However, if you have a polytunnel, January can be a very important and productive month. Because, under plastic, January and February can be your March and April. Plant now, and May and June become your premature July and August. I'm talking about bringing forward the harvest of two of my favourite vegetables – peas and broad beans – by anything up to six weeks.

This raises an important question about seasonality. Is it 'cheating' to stretch the seasons with the use of glass and plastic growing houses? Does keeping a polytunnel, which I have done with ever-increasing enthusiasm for four years now, make me a hypocrite? Am I failing to practise what I preach? Or, worse, practising a form of cultivation that, when perpetrated by others, I have tended to condemn roundly?

I don't think so. I believe that extending the growing period, if it is done by glass or plastic and without artificial heat, implies an active engagement with the seasons, not ignorance or flouting of them. And it often results in greater availability of a seasonal product at a local level. My friend, Michael Michaud, a polytunnel professional, uses his considerable skill to provide our local farm shops with some of their finest, freshest produce, including aubergines, peppers, chillies and tomatoes. These latter, incidentally, all arrive in the 'correct' season – high summer and early autumn – albeit somewhat sooner than they might have without the warmth and shelter of their polythene cocoon.

The worm turns, however (shortly before he withers and dies), with the introduction of artificial heat, artificial fertilisers, unnatural growing media, chemical pesticides and genetically modified strains. Not only does this produce crop quite outside of the normal

feb   mar   apr   may   jun   jul   aug   sep   oct   nov   dec

seasonal rhythms, it also completely defeats what in my view should be the object of the exercise – to grow quality produce in an environmentally responsible manner. It is a turning point that was reached and breached, for example, a long time ago, in much of the massive glasshouse-growing culture of Holland, which now delivers such bland and lifeless produce all year round to so many of our supermarkets.

Ultimately the proof, of course, is in the eating. Michael's tomatoes (and mine, when I manage to beat the blight) are delicious. The Dutch imports, with a few notable exceptions, are tasteless, watery and insipid. But they can travel the world without a bruise or a blemish, and sit on a supermarket shelf for a month and stay mould-free. Putting such properties before the simple matter of taste is an altogether different order of interference from stretching the seasons with a house of glass or plastic.

So I'll persist with planting my peas and beans in the polytunnel in January. And they'll be, as ever, two of my most reliable, trouble-free crops. They'll go directly into the same polytunnel beds as my winter salads came out of (I may have to whip out the last few radicchio in a line to make way for them). And when they're harvested and spent, by mid-June, the tomatoes will be transplanted from their pots into the same earth, where they'll reap the full benefit of the legumes' remarkable ability to put nitrogen back into the soil.

That's the three crop cycle for about half the beds in my polytunnel and, with a generous addition of muck and compost when the tomatoes come out, it seems to work every year.

There's one ritual harvest I look forward to this month, and sometimes I'll have the patience to wait until my birthday before I pluck one. It'll go very nicely with a glass of champagne – about five courses before the roly-poly. There aren't many things that are ripened to perfection by two months of fierce winds. Or that get better the greater the depth and variety of moulds flourishing on their skin. Or of which it can be said that the harder they become, the riper they are, and the sweeter they taste.

They shouldn't, in fact they *mustn't*, be watered. The breeze is all they need. These little beauties have been dangling under the porch, swinging like wind chimes, since early November. And now it's time to tear one down, rip its skin off and slice it up.

Salami, anyone?

Kale and chestnut soup

This is a great winter warmer, whose three principal ingredients not only are simultaneously seasonal but also complement each other beautifully: chestnuts for starch and sweetness, kale for crunch and chlorophyll, bacon for bacon's sake . . .

To serve 4

Take about 500g chestnuts, make a slit in the shell of each one and plunge them into a pan of boiling water. Bring back to the boil and simmer for 3–4 minutes. Drain, leave until cool enough to handle, then peel off the skin, including the thin, brown inner skin (or you can roast and peel the chestnuts if you prefer this way of removing the skins).

Wash and trim about 500g kale or other winter greens, cutting out and discarding the tougher stalks. Shred coarsely. Roughly dice about 250g bacon (or leftover ham) and fry gently in a little oil until just crisp.

Simmer the peeled chestnuts in around a litre of stock (poultry or game stock is best) until tender. Lift out with a slotted spoon. Mash about a quarter of the chestnuts with a fork and stir them back into the soup to thicken it a little. Roughly chop the rest of them and return to the soup. Add the kale and bacon and simmer for just 3 minutes, until the kale is lightly cooked but still fresh and green in colour. Check and adjust the seasoning.

Serve as quickly as possible, so the kale tastes nice and fresh, not 'stewed'.

- -

Grilled radicchio with melted cheese

The harsh, bitter taste of radicchio, treviso and other red chicories is not everybody's cup of tea and, to be honest, it is not always mine. But I grow them in my polytunnel anyway because, for my money, these hardy winter salad plants come into their own when thoughts of salad are banished and they are cooked for a change. The bitterness is mollified and their

feb   mar   apr   may   jun   jul   aug   sep   oct   nov   dec

natural sweetness comes to the fore. A trickle of olive oil and a generous slab of melting cheese dissipate the last traces of austerity and make this a gluttonous winter treat.

Incidentally, the dish also works well with sweeter summer lettuces such as Little Gem.

To serve 4 as starter

Cut 4 tight heads of radicchio or treviso into quarters, leaving the base of the stems intact to hold the leaves together. Brush them with olive oil and season well with salt and pepper. Then place cut-side down on a preheated heavy griddle pan – preferably the kind with raised ridges. Cook for 3–5 minutes, turning occasionally. They are ready when the outer leaves are well charred and striped from the grill and the stems are just becoming tender.

Arrange the quarters in a dish and lay thin slices of your chosen cheese over them: it might be goat's cheese or Taleggio or (a personal favourite) torta de dolcelatte. Add a few more twists of pepper and another trickle of olive oil and place in a very hot oven, or under a grill, until the cheese starts to bubble. Serve at once, 4 quarters per person.

- -

Cock pheasant au vin

Though I like to have a plump roast hen pheasant at least a couple of times during the course of the shooting season, I generally find a slow-cooked casserole is a more successful way of serving the cock birds (especially later in the season). And it's perfect for any birds that have been defrosted from frozen. This recipe pretty much follows the procedure for a classic French coq au vin – with excellent results.

To serve 6 – 8

Joint 2 oven-ready cock pheasants into 4 pieces each – i.e. 2 leg/thigh joints and 2 wing/breast joints. This is easily, if crudely, achieved by cutting the skin between leg and breast, then pushing each leg away from the body until you hear the ball and socket thigh joint tear. Then cut through any sinews still attached and follow the natural muscle contours to cut away the meat that attaches to the thigh. The remaining carcass can simply be split in half down the middle.

Heat a knob of butter and a little bacon dripping or olive oil in a heavy frying pan. Cut a 250g piece of pancetta (or thick streaky bacon) into 2cm chunks and fry gently in the fat for a few minutes until lightly browned. Transfer the bacon pieces to your chosen casserole. Then peel a dozen small onions or shallots and lightly brown them all over in the residual fat in the same pan. Transfer these to the casserole, too.

Dust the pheasant pieces lightly with seasoned flour, discarding any excess, and brown these next, turning them several times until coloured and crisp. Pour over 2 tablespoons brandy and set light to it (by tipping the pan towards the gas flame if you are cooking on gas, or with a match if you are not). When the flames have subsided, transfer the pheasant pieces and all the juices in the pan to the casserole.

Return the frying pan to the heat and deglaze it by pouring in ½ bottle of red wine, then scraping the bottom and sides of the pan while the wine bubbles. Pour the boiling wine over the pheasant and then add just enough hot stock (game, poultry or pork) or water to cover the meat. Now add a sprig of thyme, a couple of bay leaves and either 4 tablespoons home-made roast tomato purée (page 177) or 1 tablespoon concentrated tomato purée. Bring to a gentle simmer. Cover the casserole and cook at a tremulous simmer over a very low heat, or in a low oven (140°C / Gas Mark 1) for about 1¼–1½ hours, until the meat is completely tender. If you like, you can sweat 250g whole button mushrooms or sliced larger field mushrooms in a little butter until softened, then add them for the last half-hour's cooking.

Now strain the liquid into a separate clean pan, leaving the meat and vegetables in the casserole, and boil fast to reduce it by up to a half, so it forms a rich, intense sauce. If it seems a little thin, you can whisk in a few 'crumbs' of beurre manié (a paste made of equal quantities of soft butter and plain flour). Season to taste with salt and pepper.

Pour the sauce back over the pheasant and allow to bubble gently for just a few minutes before serving. Serve with plain boiled potatoes or mash and some suitable winter greens, such as kale or Savoy cabbage.

feb   mar   apr   may   jun   jul   aug   sep   oct   nov   dec

Shin of beef with macaroni

This is really a procedure to make a variety of hearty, soupy stews to warm your toes in bleak weather. It could easily be adapted to make a rabbit stew, or a mutton broth. Whatever your principal ingredients, you'll end up with meltingly tender meat in a thin but very tasty juice. Bolstered with macaroni, and eaten in a bowl to catch plenty of the well-flavoured liquor, it makes a perfect one-pot winter supper.

You can either use beef stock in this dish or you can simply add the shin bone to the pot and use water. But if the latter, you will have to skim off the dirty bubbles that rise to the surface for the first 30 minutes or so of simmering. Discard the bone at the end of cooking, but not until you have scooped out the marrow and added it, in quivering little pieces, to the stew.

To serve 6

Cut a kilo of shin of beef into thick strips. Cut 250g salted pork belly or pancetta into chunky cubes. Heat a little olive oil or dripping in a large, heavy frying pan. Gently fry the pork until it is lightly browned and the fat runs. Transfer to a casserole, but leave the pan and bacon-flavoured oil on the heat. Now brown the shin meat in the same pan, in batches, transferring it to the casserole as soon as it is lightly coloured. Finally slice 2 onions and sweat them in the same pan without allowing them to colour. Transfer to the casserole when soft and translucent. Add a couple of large carrots, peeled and in big chunks, a few sticks of celery, sliced, a couple of bay leaves and a sprig of thyme. Pour over a few cups of beef stock, adding a little water if you need it – the meat should be covered by a good couple of centimetres. (Or add the bone and just cover with water as discussed above.) Season sparingly with salt and pepper.

Bring to a simmer and cook, uncovered, at a very low, tremulous simmer for 2–3 hours, until the meat is completely tender. You can cook it in a slow oven (about 140°C/Gas Mark 1), if you like. Check and adjust the seasoning.

Cook 250g small macaroni, risoni (rice-shaped pasta) or other soup-friendly pasta separately and add to the casserole just before serving. Serve in warmed bowls, with plenty of the juice ladled over.

Roast cod's head, gigot style

I love this dish, as it feels as if you're getting something from nothing. In fact, on a good-sized cod's head there is easily enough meat to serve four generously, especially if it has been cut with this dish in mind, to include a little 'shoulder'. You may notice that the treatment it gets — studded with garlic and herbs — is exactly like a leg of lamb. Hence the 'gigot style'.

You can mete out the same treatment to the heads of other large white fish, such as halibut, coley and big John Dory.

To serve 2 — 6 (depending on the size of the head)

Ask the fishmonger (or fisherman) for the head of a large (4–10 kilo) cod, cut generously so there's a bit of meat on the 'shoulders'. You should get it at a rock-bottom price. If you're buying a bunch of other stuff, you might get it for nothing.

At home, rinse the head thoroughly and pat dry. Massage the whole head with olive oil. Make small incisions wherever you see a fleshy part of the head and stuff in little slivers of garlic and small sprigs of rosemary and/or thyme. Stick a bay leaf in the fish's mouth. Grind plenty of black pepper over the head and sprinkle it generously with flaky sea salt. Trickle a bit more olive oil over it. Place in a hot oven (220°C/Gas Mark 7) for 30–50 minutes, depending on the size of the head. You can baste the head with its oily juices once or twice during cooking. It should end up blistered and crisp, almost burnt in parts.

There is no dainty way to eat the head. Forks, and fingers when it's cool enough to touch, should be deployed to pick as much meat as possible from all over the head, including the cheeks, lips and below the gill plates. You will find tasty little scallops of flesh in all sorts of unexpected places. And the skin, crispy, salty and garlicky, is to be fought over. I like to serve it with mashed potato.

feb   mar   apr   may   jun   jul   aug   sep   oct   nov   dec

Woodcock (or snipe) on toast

For game aficionados, this is one of the ultimate treats. Traditionally the insides of the birds are not removed before cooking but left in, then spread on a piece of toast on which the bird is served. This is not just a piece of macho posturing: the flavour of the intestines isn't strong at all, but creamy and mildly liverish. What is macho and, I think, foolish is hanging game to the point of rottenness: 3–5 days, or a week in cold weather, is more than enough to develop flavour and tenderness in these little birds.

If you can get hold of woodcock and snipe – and you may have to order them – it's worth overcoming any scepticism to try this fabulous dish. Traditionally, one woodcock, or two snipe, per person makes a robust starter. Supplemented with game chips and greens, the same would content many as a main course.

The only thing that needs to be removed from the plucked bird before roasting is the gizzard. If you are buying your birds, you could ask the butcher or game dealer to do this. But it's very easy: with the point of a sharp knife, make a small slit in the vent end of the bird. Insert your little finger and feel around. The first little hard lump you come to is the gizzard. Once you've located it, spear it with a cocktail stick or needle and gently pull it out. It will have a trail of intestine attached. Snip it off and push the intestine back inside the cavity. This is the kind of operation you'll either enjoy, or you won't.

Preheat the oven to 230°C/Gas Mark 8 (or, if your oven doesn't reach that, heat it as high as it will go and cook the birds for a few extra minutes). Massage a little soft butter into the breast of each woodcock or snipe and season with a little salt and freshly ground black pepper. Lay some streaky bacon over the breast of each bird – ½ a rasher for a snipe, 2 halves for a woodcock. Tuck the head and neck of each bird (if they are still intact) under its wing. Place the birds in a roasting tin and roast for 8–20 minutes, depending on how pink you like your meat: 8 minutes is about right for a medium-rare snipe, 20 for a well-done woodcock. Remove the bacon after about 5 minutes and take it out of the oven.

When the birds come out of the oven, transfer them to a warmed plate – they'll rest for about 10 minutes while you sort out the intestines. Scoop these carefully out of the cavity of the birds with a teaspoon. Unless the birds are very well done, they will still be quite pink and bloody. In a small frying pan, heat a little butter and add the bacon you took from the birds, chopped fairly finely. Sizzle for a minute or two, then add the contents of the birds' cavities – intestines, hearts, livers, the lot – and any juices from the roasting tin. Add just a little red wine and/or port – a teaspoon or two for each bird. Bubble gently for a couple of minutes, mashing the lumpy bits with a fork, and season sparingly with salt and pepper, then remove from the heat.

Make and lightly butter a small round of toast for each bird. On each piece of toast, put a heap of the warm 'pâté' on one side and a roast bird on the other. Serve at once, with the very best red wine.

Guests should be allowed – indeed, encouraged – to pick up the birds and gnaw every last scrap of meat off the bone. Even the heads can be split, and the tiny, pea-sized brains sucked out – a grisly treat perhaps, but one the enthusiast would never forego. If you enjoyed the bit with the intestines, you'll probably be up for it by now.

- -

Three (or more) root mash

This is a luxurious, comforting mash that goes well with roast joints in winter but is also delicious as a supper dish on its own – or maybe with a couple of rashers of bacon and a fried egg on top! It can also be spun into some fine variations, as described.

To serve 4

Peel and chop equal quantities (about 500g) of potatoes and 2 (or more) of the following: carrots, parsnips, celeriac and swede. Cook the potatoes in one pan and the other roots together in another, simmering them all in lightly salted water until completely tender. Drain and return to the pans to steam off for a few minutes.

In the larger of the 2 pans, heat a good 125g butter with a little milk and cream if you like, seasoning with black pepper and grated nutmeg. Add the potatoes and mash

feb   mar   apr   may   jun   jul   aug   sep   oct   nov   dec

until smooth. Rub the other root vegetables through a sieve, or process in a machine, and put into the same pan as the potatoes. Beat well until thoroughly mixed, adding more hot milk and butter, if needed, to get a nice, loose consistency. Taste and adjust the seasoning.

The mash can be kept warm in a low oven, covered with buttered foil, but not for more than an hour or so, or it will start to dry out.

Variations

Three-root soup

There is a point at which a mash becomes a purée, and a point at which a purée becomes a soup. Both these points are worth exploring with this dish. If I'm setting out to make the soup version, I'll usually cook the roots (but not the potatoes) in stock rather than water, and use a little less butter for mashing. Then I'll save the stock when I drain the vegetables and use it to thin the mash to a thick soup consistency. This sieved soup definitely beats a liquidised soup, as the blender will make any mixture with potatoes in it turn a little gluey.

Jerusalem artichoke soup

This is one of the best of all winter soups, but there's no getting away from the fact that it will make you fart. Make as for three-root soup, using peeled Jerusalem artichokes to make up at least half of the root vegetables. Don't add nutmeg, but use plenty of black pepper. Finish the soup with a trickle of olive oil or, if you're feeling flash, truffle or mushroom oil.

- -

Salsify gratin

Salsify, and its interchangeable black-skinned relative, scorzonera, are two really terrific, yet criminally underrated root vegetables. But not for long, I suspect. Chefs are cottoning on to their unique, almost oystery flavour, and there are already signs that the supermarkets are

feb   mar   apr   may   jun   jul   aug   sep   oct   nov   dec

singling them out for special treatment as something 'new and trendy'. Of course, they are nothing of the kind, but good old-fashioned English root vegetables that were popular for centuries and only went out of favour after the First World War. I don't begrudge them a bit of slick marketing, though, because they really deserve a comeback.

They are very good simply boiled and buttered. Simmered in stock and puréed until velvety smooth, they make excellent soup. But my personal favourite is this delectable gratin, which I like to serve solo, as a starter.

To serve 4

Wash and peel 1 kilo (unwashed weight) salsify or scorzonera, placing it in water acidulated with a little lemon juice to prevent it discolouring. Some roots are more or less equally thin all the way along. Others will be more tapered, like parsnips. Cut up the thicker ends so they are in long batons about the same thickness as the thin ends. Cover with lightly salted water, bring to the boil and simmer for about 15 minutes, until just tender.

Drain well, arrange in a single layer in a buttered shallow gratin dish, then season with plenty of black pepper and trickle over 2–3 tablespoons double cream. Sprinkle over a handful of breadcrumbs and bake in a fairly hot oven (200°C/Gas Mark 6) for 20 minutes, until crusty and browned on top. Serve piping hot.

- -

Tipsy fruity roly-poly

Of all the classic British suet puddings, a roly-poly has to be one of the easiest to make, and one of the most irresistible to eat. It's basically a suet swiss roll. The filling can be anything seasonal, personal or suitable that comes to hand — see my suggested variations. This filling, of rum, ginger and raisins, is a particular winter favourite of mine.

If the rolling and wrapping of the roly-poly sound complicated, then the picture sequence on pages 40–41 should demystify the process, which is actually very simple.

To serve 8

First prepare the filling. Chop 100g preserved ginger in syrup into pea-sized pieces. Put them in a bowl with 500g best-quality plump, seedless raisins. Heat a wine glass of rum and 2 tablespoons of syrup from the preserved ginger until just simmering, then pour it over the raisins and leave to plump up and infuse – ideally a good couple of hours (or even overnight). Stir them up a couple of times while waiting.

Pour off the rummy liquid into a small, clean pan, add a good tablespoon of sugar and a couple of tablespoons of water and stir over a low heat until dissolved. Then bring to the boil and simmer for 5 minutes to get a fairly viscous syrup. Pour this back over the raisins.

Mix 250g suet with 500g self-raising flour and a pinch of salt. Make a well in the centre and gradually add about 300ml cold water, working it in with a fork, then with your hands, to get a stiff but manageable dough. Shape the dough roughly into a square and roll it out on a well-floured surface into a rectangle no more than 1cm thick. Spread the syrupy fruit in an even layer all over the suet pastry, leaving a 4cm margin round the edges. Fold these margins towards the centre, then roll up the pastry away from you. Use a wet thumb to make a sticky seal on the end of the pastry, so your roly-poly doesn't come unstuck.

Now wrap the roly-poly in a wet tea towel and tie it with string at either end like a Christmas cracker. Cook in a fish kettle or a large saucepan of gently simmering water for 3 hours, topping up the water as necessary. (It doesn't have to be completely submerged, but should be two-thirds covered with the water.) Unwrap carefully, cut into thick slices and serve with hot custard.

Variations

Once you've mastered the basic technique, the roly-poly is a dish that begs to be customised. Jam roly-poly is a classic, of course, and the best jam to make it with is raspberry. My plum jampote (page 189) also makes a superb filling. And the booze and dried fruit theme can be taken in all sorts of directions – whisky and apricot, prunes and Armagnac, even dried bananas and Baileys? Maybe not!

feb   mar   apr   may   jun   jul   aug   sep   oct   nov   dec

FEBRUARY _____

I hate February. Basically, it's a month longer than I'm prepared to tolerate of bone-chilling, icy winds and strength-sapping seasonal motionlessness.

So if anyone would like to offer me a couple of weeks' fishing and diving in tropical seas for the last two weeks of February every year for the rest of my life, they could certainly have a small piece of my soul – ideally the piece February has spent 28 days of every year for the last 38 years trying to destroy.

Of course, the February effect is largely psychological, because the weather is often much better than in March – when it usually rains a lot more and blows a lot more. February, by contrast, can produce quite a few of those steely-blue sunny days without a breath of wind. These are not to be squandered. Get outside, with a thick jersey on but no coat, and walk with your back to the sun. Feel that faint glow as the wool warms up and your skin starts to tingle. Out in the field I can see my sheep doing the same. I wonder if they are thinking, albeit sheepishly, the same thing as me: it doesn't really penetrate but at least it's there – real sunshine, and a sanity-saving promise of spring.

I don't do much in the garden in February, because there isn't much to be done. The plants, like all the sensible animals, are hibernating. Dormancy is, however, something the gardener can take advantage of. Sleeping plants can still be moved, carefully, without complaint. But don't hang about. The sap seems to be rising earlier and earlier each year.

The range of winter vegetables is beginning to dwindle. It's time to take what remains, banish thoughts of frugality and asceticism and tart it up as something really special. Explore the more exotic possibilities of the humble potato by making Jansson's temptation (page 52).

Have you been as adventurous as you might have been with the versatile parsnip? If you've already made Richard's parsnip risotto (page 221), and enjoyed the collision of parsnip with Parmesan, try serving a plate of piping-hot, olive-oil-roasted parsnip chunks with Parmesan shavings – so good it works as a dish on its own.

It is in the kitchen that the battle against February must be fought and, if not won, then perhaps, in a good year, honourably drawn. The skill is to feed the family so warmly that the inherent meanness of the month goes largely unnoticed. The central heating and comfort factors of the food – by which I mean sugar and fat, as well as starchy carbohydrates – can be subtly (or even unsubtly) upped.

But wasn't I already urging you to comfort cook in January? Since November, in fact? Of course. Since winter-fuel food has already been on the menu for a few months, the question is, how do you up the ante on the comfort stakes at this late stage – without simply pouring treacle and lard down the throats of your loved ones? It can be done. Winter soups and stews can incorporate noodles or dumplings, or be given a crust and become pies, or suet puddings. An annual outing for such classics as Sussex pond pudding, or spotted dick, or a roly-poly (page 38) will be most welcome at this time of year.

Comfort food doesn't have to be time-consuming. Think of pancakes. They must rank as the easiest and speediest comfort food you can make (after toast, I suppose). Shrove Tuesday usually falls in February but we hardly need this excuse to make pancakes. I have a French wife and a four-year-old son who loves cooking, and whenever a chill wind creeps under the kitchen door a cry goes up, '*Allons faire des crêpes.*'

I love the ritual of cooking them and eating them, taking it in turns ('Me next, me next!'), watching the creamy white batter set firm in the pan, and trying to resolve the tantalising question of what to have on the next one. Sometimes we gorge ourselves silly, putting various toppings on the table and getting the pancake production line motoring till even the greediest, goggliest-eyed child (that's Oscar) can't manage another one.

When it comes to making the batter, Marie scoffs at the idea of measuring any ingredients – so the brackets that follow are mine. She simply tips a pile of plain flour (200g) into a bowl, breaks 3 eggs into the middle and starts beating. Little by little she adds enough milk (about 500ml) to get the consistency she likes – roughly that of single cream.

feb   mar   apr   may   jun   jul   aug   sep   oct   nov   dec

The pan for cooking doesn't have to be a dedicated crêpe pan (they have almost no sides, for ease of turning), but it must be truly non-stick. It should be heated until very hot – though not actually smoking. The merest smear of butter or oil over the pan before each pancake does the job. A ladle is the best tool for pouring batter into the pan, which must be tilted and turned to spread it evenly over the surface. If it's immediately apparent that there is too much batter, you can, as soon as the pan is coated, tip the excess back into the bowl. This creates a lip of batter up one edge of the pan, which some may regard as unaesthetic but the true enthusiast will recognise as a bonus because it is, simply, more pancake.

The pancake is ready to turn when a lifted edge reveals the underside to be lightly tanned. Marie wouldn't dream of tossing hers. She has a wide metal spatula with which she effortlessly flips it. I will occasionally risk ridicule and attempt a toss.

A scant minute on the B-side is usually enough to finish the pancake. I love the fact that the side that is cooked second looks so different from the one that is cooked first. Instead of an even, golden tan, it has dark brown speckles, where the bubbles formed on the surface of side one have hit the hot pan first on the flip.

Generally, I like my pancake served speckled side up. Then again, if it's speckled side down and you roll it up, the spots are on the outside of the roll, and that's nice too. It's a tough call. But I'm definitely a roller, not a folder.

My first pancake of any given session is always topped with a sprinkling of caster sugar, a squeeze of lemon juice and nothing else. This is invariably such a pleasant experience as to merit a repeat. Meanwhile Oscar usually reaches for the raspberry jam, while Marie favours Nutella (chocolate and hazelnut spread) – a French classic.

On Shrove Tuesday itself, more elaborate and over-the-top fillings may be wheeled out. Banana and toffee is my all-time favourite, made cheatily by melting some good-quality toffees in a little milk, then pouring this sauce over a sliced ripe banana laid along the pancake.

A tart compote of Bramley apples, still available from store, with a sprinkling of brown sugar and a dollop of double or even clotted cream, is another wonderful concoction.

Pancakes will always be comfort food of the highest order, as much because of the ritual of the session as the eating of the end product. In fact, it takes a long time to tire of either. By the time you do, it will practically be spring.

Smoky cheaty brandade

Brandade, the classic Provençal salt cod dish, is one of the all-time great comfort foods – salty, creamy, oily, garlicky, it hits so many oral pleasure spots it's just irresistible. An authentic brandade, however, involves first finding some authentic salt cod, soaking it for anything up to 48 hours, then cooking it and picking out the skin and bones – and that's before you even get round to making it.

Luckily it is possible to make a delectable version of the dish using a much more familiar and convenient product – smoked haddock or cod (or the increasingly available smoked pollack). Purists might not approve, but really they shouldn't moan, as this version of the dish is very much in the spirit of the original – fishy, garlicky, rich, indulgent. Tasting it would, I feel, quickly shut them up.

To serve 4 as a main course, 8 as a starter or 12 as a canapé

Poach a 500g piece of smoked haddock or cod fillet in just enough whole milk to cover it. About 5 minutes should do it, then remove from the heat and let it cool in the milk. Boil about 500g peeled potatoes (mashing type) in lightly salted water until tender, then drain. Mash thoroughly with a good knob of butter and enough of the milk from poaching the fish to get a soft but not sloppy mash. Pick over the fish, discarding the skin and any bones. Heat 4 tablespoons best olive oil in a small pan over a low heat. Finely chop 2–3 large cloves of garlic and sweat them gently in the oil for 2–3 minutes, without letting them colour.

Put the flaked fish in a food processor and pulse several times, trickling in the warm garlic and olive oil as you do so (or, more traditionally, pound everything together in a large pestle and mortar). Then add another 2–3 tablespoons olive oil, and 1–2 tablespoons double cream if you're feeling really greedy, and pulse/pound again. Add a little of the poaching milk, if necessary, to give a mixture the consistency of mashed potato. Now combine the fish mixture with the potato, beating thoroughly so they are well mixed together. (There are various low- and high-tech ways you can combine all the ingredients, but don't at any point process the potatoes in a machine, as it makes them gluey and spoils the texture of the dish.) Season to taste with black pepper – it probably won't need salt.

When you want to serve the brandade, spread it in an ovenproof dish and bake for 15–20 minutes in a fairly hot oven (190°C/Gas Mark 5), until piping hot. Serve as a starter or canapé, on or with suitable slices of toast, or as a main course, with toast and winter salads and/or braised leeks, greens or chicory.

- -

Leeky Welsh rarebit

A good Welsh rarebit is so much more than cheese on toast. It's quick-fix comfort food of the highest order, and a great dish with which to confront a cold snap. It's an easy recipe to improvise once you get the knack, but worth having fixed quantities to get you started. The addition of leeks is quite optional but it is very delicious, and makes more of a meal of it. And it also helps to make sense of the Welsh sobriquet.

To serve 4 – 6

If you fancy the leeky option, wash and finely slice a couple of leeks and sweat them in a little butter and oil for about 10 minutes, until tender but not coloured.

For the cheese mixture, melt 50g butter in a small saucepan over a low heat, then stir in 50g plain flour to make a thick roux. Cook for a couple of minutes, stirring to prevent the roux burning. Stir in 300ml hot beer (bitter or pale ale, not lager) by degrees, until you have a very thick, smooth sauce. Add 150g mature Cheddar, grated, and stir until melted. You should now have a thick paste. Season well with a blob of English mustard, a good splash of Worcestershire sauce and a few twists of black pepper. Now stir the leeks into the mixture if you're using them.

Lightly toast 6 thick slices of bread, then pile up the cheesy mixture on each slice. Flash under a hot grill for a few minutes, until browned and bubbling.

Jansson's temptation

It's amazing what you can do with a few potatoes and a tin of anchovies. Plus maybe a bit of cream . . . This is a classic Swedish dish and a great winter warmer.

To serve 2 for supper

Open a tin of anchovies and trickle the oil from it into a pan. Slice a large onion and fry it in the oil until softened. Peel a couple of spuds (about 400–500g) and cut them into thick matchsticks/very thin chips. Add them to the onion and sweat until they start to soften. Take off the heat and stir in 4 tablespoons double cream and the anchovies. Season with black pepper. Spread the mixture in a small gratin dish and bake in a hot oven (200°C/Gas Mark 6) for 35 45 minutes, until crusty and crispy and utterly irresistible.

- -

Spaghetti cheese soufflé

This is a cunning way of transforming a regular cheese soufflé into a hearty winter supper dish. Caerphilly is an excellent cooking cheese, to use with Cheddar or on its own. Or use a mixture of Gruyère and Parmesan.

To serve 4

Break 100g spaghetti into lengths of a few inches and boil in salted water until *al dente*. Drain and toss in a few drops of olive oil to prevent sticking. Melt 50g butter in a heavy saucepan and stir in 50g plain flour to make a roux. Cook for a minute or so, then add 300ml hot milk by degrees, stirring until you have a thick, smooth béchamel. Allow to simmer gently for just a minute, then take off the heat. Add 150g grated Cheddar or Caerphilly (or, for a change, a mixture of Gruyère and Parmesan) and stir until melted.

Beat 3 egg yolks into the cheese mixture. Stir in the cooked spaghetti until thoroughly incorporated. Season well with black pepper, and salt if necessary.

Whisk 4 egg whites until stiff and fold them gently but thoroughly into the mixture. Transfer to 2 medium soufflé dishes or 1 large one and cook at 190°C/Gas Mark 5 for 25–30 minutes, until well risen and golden. Serve immediately.

- -

Steak and kidney pudding

This must be the ultimate trencherman's winter warmer. You don't have to pre-cook the filling – there are many recipes for this dish that instruct you to put raw meat into the pudding and steam it for up to 5 hours. But I prefer this method, as you can get the gravy and seasonings just how you like them. The suet crust cooks through in 2 hours, no problem.

To serve 6

First make the filling. Trim and cut into large cubes a kilo of beef skirt, shin or chuck. Cut up and remove the cores from about 500g beef kidneys. Season 50g plain flour well with salt and pepper. Heat a little fat or oil in a large, heavy frying pan until fairly hot but not smoking. With floured hands, toss a couple of handfuls of beef in the seasoned flour, then put it in the pan. Brown well on all sides, then transfer to a large saucepan. Brown all the meat like this, including the kidneys, in batches to avoid overcrowding the pan.

When all the meat is browned, deglaze the empty pan with a glass of red wine, stirring and scraping up any burnt, crispy bits with the edge of a spatula. Add the deglazed juices to the meat in the saucepan. Heat a little more fat or oil in the now-clean frying pan, add 1 large or 2 medium onions, sliced, and sweat for a few minutes, until softened. Add to the meat. Add a scant tablespoon of tomato ketchup, a teaspoon of good English mustard, a bay leaf and about 750ml beef stock or water (it should barely cover the meat). Stir gently and bring to a subtle, tremulous simmer. Cook for about 1½ hours, until

feb mar apr may jun jul aug sep oct nov dec

the beef is fairly tender but not 'finished'. It is going to get another couple of hours in the pudding. Note that skirt and shin will take a little longer than chuck steak. Check the seasoning towards the end of cooking and adjust as necessary.

At this stage the filling can be left, covered, in the fridge for a day or two. Or it can be very successfully frozen. If you like mushrooms in your steak and kidney pudding, gently fry about 250g whole button mushrooms or sliced larger mushrooms in a little fat or oil for a few minutes to let the juices run, then add to the filling before you make up the pudding (they will cook through in the pudding).

Now make the suet crust. Mix 250g beef suet with 500g self-raising flour and a pinch of salt. Add cold water by degrees (up to about 300ml may be necessary) until you have a workable dough that is not too sticky. Set aside about a third for the lid and shape the remaining two-thirds into a ball. Roll out on a floured surface to about 1.5cm thick and use to line a greased pudding basin of about 1.5 litres capacity. Pile in the meat with its gravy. Roll out the lid piece. Wet the edges of the lining crust and place the lid over it, pressing firmly with your thumb to stick the lid to the lining.

Fold a double layer of greaseproof paper to include a pleat, allowing for expansion of the suet crust while the pudding is steamed. Tie the paper over the top of the pudding basin, then tie up the whole basin in muslin or a cotton cloth, if you like, to make it easier to raise and lower into the pan. Place on an upturned saucer inside a large pan of simmering water that comes a third of the way up the basin. Steam, with the saucepan lid slightly ajar, for 2 hours, topping up with boiling water from the kettle to stop the pan boiling dry.

Unwrap the pudding basin and run a palette knife carefully round the edge to loosen the pudding. Place a warmed plate over the top and invert the basin. Give it a shake to turn out the pudding. It should hold its shape – at least until you cut the first slice!

Serve with steamed seasonal greens, such as Savoy cabbage, winter greens or Brussels sprouts, and good English mustard. On a cold February day a real trencherman could no doubt manage a dollop of good buttery mash as well.

Variation: Steak and kidney pie

Make the same filling, cook it for an extra 45 minutes, and bake as for game pie (page 56).

Rough puff pastry

February is a good month for pies, and the easiest way to make a good pie is to make a stew with a nice thick gravy and simply bake it under a lid of pastry. For a more full-on affair, you'll want to line the pie dish with pastry too. Of course you can buy pastry, but if you want to make a bit of a project of your pie, and particularly if you have kids who can help with the mixing and rolling, then a home-made pie crust is a deeply satisfying achievement. So here's a recipe for the best pie pastry I know. Whatever you put on the inside, I guarantee the outside won't disappoint!

The quantity below will generously line *and* cover a large (1.5 litre) pie dish, with trimmings to spare for decorations and even a few jam tarts or an apple turnover.

Sift 500g plain flour into a mixing bowl with a pinch of salt. Cut 250g cold butter or lard into walnut-sized pieces and toss them in the flour until coated. Then add a little ice-cold water, bringing the dough together with your hands and adding no more water than you need to get a medium-firm dough that is not too sticky, with large pieces of the fat still intact in it.

On a well-floured surface, shape the dough into a fat rectangle and roll it out with a well-floured rolling pin, rolling away from you in one direction only to keep the rectangular shape as far as you can. When the dough is 2cm thick (or less), fold the far third towards you and fold the near third back over that (i.e. you now have a rectangle a third the size and 3 times as thick). Turn the pastry a quarter turn (90 degrees) to the right and roll it out again, away from you, into another long rectangle.

Repeat this procedure, folding and turning, at least 4 times, preferably 5 or 6. You will need to keep dusting with more flour and, should the dough become too loose or sticky (a danger in warm or damp weather), chill it in the fridge for an hour or so, then dust with more flour and resume rolling. At any rate, the finished pastry should be folded up for a final time and chilled for at least 1 hour before rolling out and using.

feb   mar   apr   may   jun   jul   aug   sep   oct   nov   dec

Game pie

Game pie is by definition an improvised dish, to be filled with whatever selection of furred or feathered game comes to hand. For those who shoot, February is a good month to make a fine pie from game that has accumulated in the freezer. For those who are buying their game, there are often great bargains to be had from butchers who also have a stockpile of frozen game that they would like to clear.

Include a pig's trotter in the stock and the filling of your pie will set into a delicious gamy jelly, which makes it a fantastic dish to eat cold. With this in mind, the pie juices in this recipe are clear, but if you want a thicker gravy for a hot pie, then toss the game pieces in flour before frying.

To serve 6

Prepare a selection of game that might comprise, for example, a rabbit, skinned and jointed, a pheasant, oven-ready and jointed, a couple of pigeons, left whole. Cut about 100g pancetta or streaky bacon into large, chunky dice. Heat a little fat or oil in a large, heavy frying pan and fry gently until nicely browned. Then transfer to your waiting stockpot, leaving the fat in the pan. Brown the game pieces (floured first, if you like — see above), a few at a time, in the frying pan, transferring them to the stockpot as they are done.

Pour any excess fat out of the pan, then replace on the heat and deglaze by stirring in a glass of red wine. Pour the deglazed pan juices into the stockpot. Add a pig's trotter (if you fancy the option of a cold pie) and some stock vegetables (say, 2 carrots, 2 onions and a couple of sticks of celery, roughly chopped), plus a bay leaf and a sprig of thyme (but no salt or pepper just yet). Pour over just enough water to cover. Bring gently to the boil and simmer at a slow tremble for about an hour.

Fish out the game pieces and the bacon with a slotted spoon and leave until cool enough to handle. Pick off all the meat from the bones with your fingers, breaking it up into generous, pie-friendly pieces. Return the bones and skin to the stockpot and continue to simmer gently for at least another hour, more if you have time. Then strain off the stock and taste it. You can reduce it to concentrate the flavour if you like, but you will need at least

500ml for your pie. Season to taste when you are happy with its strength. If you have cooked the stock long enough, you can pick off the tender meat and gelatinous skin from the pig's trotter and add that to the game meat.

Cut 500g bought or home-made pastry (the rough puff pastry on page 55 is perfect) into 2 rectangles, one very slightly bigger than the other. Roll out the larger piece to about 5mm thick and use to line a lightly greased pie dish, about 1.2 litres in capacity. Take the pastry right to the edge of the flat lip of the dish, trimming off the excess. Roll out the smaller piece so it will more than cover the top of the pie. Spoon in the meat until it is at least level with the top of the dish, preferably mounding it just a little higher. Ladle in enough of the stock to come 2cm short of the top of the pie – i.e. not quite covering the meat.

Brush the edges of the pastry with a little beaten egg and cover the pie with the rolled-out lid piece, crimping the edges with your thumb so the lid is well glued down to the lining. Make up any decorations with the pastry trimmings – leaves, a rabbit's head, your initials, a twelve-bore – and stick them on with more beaten egg. Then brush the remaining egg all over the surface of the pie. Make 2 x-shaped vent holes in the pastry at either end of the pie. Bake in a moderately hot oven (190°C/Gas Mark 5) for about 50 minutes–1 hour, until the pastry is puffed up and golden brown.

To serve the pie, cut wedges right through the lining pastry at the bottom of the dish so everyone (at least everyone who wants it) gets a mixture of sticky bottom pastry and crispy lid pastry with their meat. Serve hot with mash and braised celery or steamed buttered cabbage. Or serve cold (trotter version) with pickles and salad.

Variation: Game pudding

Fans of the suet pudding can make a wonderful game pudding instead of a pie by preparing the filling in exactly the same way, then using it instead of the steak and kidney filling in the recipe on page 53. I hope you're beginning to appreciate the improvisational possibilities with these pies and puddings!

Rice pudding with butterscotch apples

Thanks to the school version (out of an enormous tin, I suspect), I used to hate rice pudding. Only recently did I discover how sublime it can be. It's easy, too, the secret being in the occasional stir that helps separate the grains, and the half-and-half mix of milk and cream.

There are all sorts of treats and toppings to serve with the perfect rice pudding, such as hot jam, or booze-soaked dried fruits (rum and raisins, prune and Armagnac, apricots and whisky, for example). The simple toffee sauce described for pancakes on page 46 is also divine with rice pudding, as are melted Mars bars! But these 'butterscotch apples', an experiment a few years back, have become a great favourite.

To serve 6

Melt 50g unsalted butter in a saucepan over a low heat and add 100g pudding rice, stirring so it is coated with the butter (it shouldn't fry or even so much as sizzle). Add 500ml whole milk mixed with 500ml double cream and stir in 50g caster sugar. Stir for a couple of minutes to warm the milk and dissolve the sugar. Transfer to a buttered deep ovenproof dish and grate a little nutmeg over the surface if you like. Place in a slow oven (140°C/Gas Mark 1) and cook for 3–3½ hours, opening the oven door every 30 minutes or so to stir the pudding gently from the bottom to the top, separating the grains and working the surface skin back into the pudding. When the rice has expanded to fill the dish and is quite tender (2½–3 hours should do it), leave without stirring for the last half-hour so it can form a nice, golden-brown skin. Turn the oven up to 170°C/Gas Mark 3 for the last 10 minutes. You can even give it a flash under the grill if you like.

Prepare the butterscotch apples. Peel and core 4–5 firm, tart eating apples (about 400–500g); Cox's or Granny Smiths are perfect, as they have good acidity and keep their shape when cooked. Cut them into 1–2cm dice. Melt 50g unsalted butter in a large frying pan and fry the apples very gently. After a couple of minutes, sprinkle over 50g light brown sugar. Keep tossing and gently frying the apples until they are tender and lightly coated in a buttery, sugary, appley glaze (about 12–15 minutes in all). Serve hot from the pan, beside a generous dollop of the hot rice pudding.

feb   mar   apr   may   jun   jul   aug   sep   oct   nov   dec

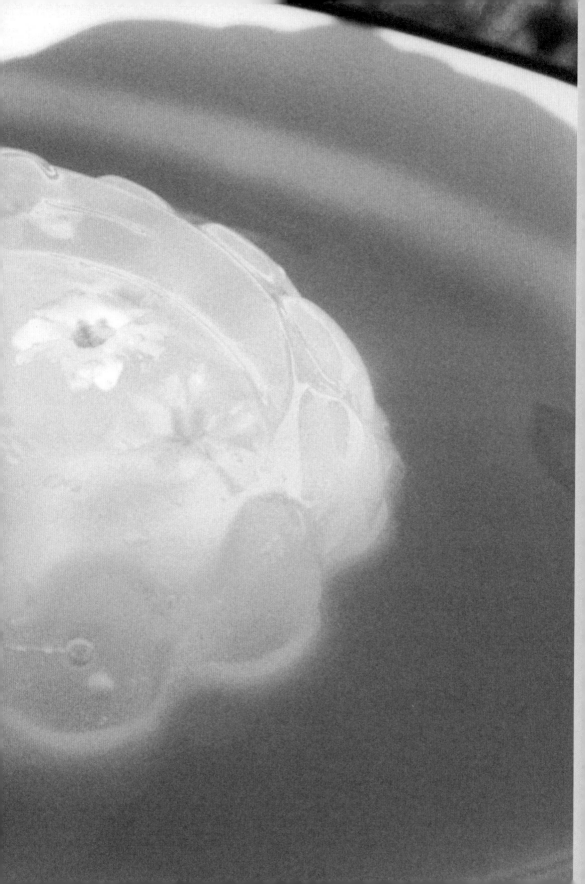

MARCH_____

For most of its 31 days March can be every bit as miserable, marrow-chilling and monotonous as February. But it doesn't matter, because March has something that February lacks: hope.

This expresses itself in a number of small but irrepressible details. However cold and wet it gets, and stays, various life-enhancing things are sure to have happened by the end of the month. Primroses will defy the harshest of weather with their unambiguously springy splash of yellow. Likewise the daffodils. You may be waiting a couple of months yet for sleeveless tops and short skirts but in the garden at least, spring is showing a leg.

Another reward for your patience is a calendar event that for me is always one of the most thrilling days of the year. I mean that last Sunday of the month when the clocks go forward. An hour less in bed, some people moan. A negligible price to pay, I would suggest, for somewhere in the region of 210 extra hours of evening light over the coming months (I just worked it out). That's nearly ten whole days' worth of hours to spend gardening, fishing, barbecuing, picnicking and generally outdoorsing it. Weather permitting, of course.

One thing that surprises me every March (you'd think I'd be getting used to it by now) is how the hedgerow plants, despite competing furiously with each other on soil that's a whole lot stonier and a lot less muck-rich than mine, steal such a march (a March?) on my lovingly tended seedlings. The wild chervil (aka cow parsley), nettles and alexanders are all half a yard out of the ground before my carrots and spinach have shown a couple of inches. Of course it's not really a 'despite' but a 'because of'. You've got to be an early starter, and a tough one, to stand a chance in that jungle. I've long since given up being 'jealous' on behalf of my cultivated protégés. My motto has become 'if you can't beat them, eat them'.

Of all the wild spring greens, nettles are perhaps the most reliable early-March croppers – and, of course, the most easily identifiable. What four-year-old has not been taught to recognise and avoid their vicious, serrated sting? Actually, my four-year-old has been taught to put on a stout pair of gloves and go out with his scissors to cut them for the kitchen. He has thereby learned 'respect' for this irrepressible plant in two senses of the word.

The tiniest young nettles have tender stalks, and can be snipped just above the ground and used whole. As the plants become more vigorous, just the crown of leaves at the top should be harvested. As spring turns to summer, the nettles soon become coarse, flowerheads begin to form and they quickly run to seed. These specimens are not good eating. But where nettles have been strimmed or mown, fresh young growth will appear within a few weeks, and this can be treated like the early spring plants.

I can't emphasise enough how worthwhile nettles are as a vegetable. Freshly gathered, with just a pick over for lurking protein, and a quick rinse, they are ready to make one of my favourite green soups (see *The River Cottage Cookbook*). They can also be used as a straight swap for spinach in such classic dishes as *gnocchi verde* and creamed spinach (page 116). And I have recently discovered that they make a classy risotto, especially if combined with sorrel (page 73).

When you're blanching nettles for such dishes, or preparing them as a vegetable, don't discard the cooking water. It's effectively a strong nettle tea. Sweeten with honey, sharpen with a squeeze of lemon, and drink as a fortifying brew. Nettles are rich in iron, formic and silicic acid and natural histamines – a healthy spring tonic if ever there was one.

There are other wild spring greens to look out for. This is the month to start gathering sea spinach (to be used exactly like its garden descendant), alexanders and hogweed shoots (both of whose fleshy stems can be served like asparagus). Watercress can be had, too, at the edge of streams and trickling ditches. And try laying a few young leaves of wild garlic on top of a slab of Cheddar in a doorstep cheese sandwich.

In the garden it is future, not present, harvests that occupy my thoughts. On a large table in the polytunnel, formed out of two old doors propped on top of trestles, the summer's vegetable-garden-to-be is laid out in miniature. I don't mean as a scale model (I'm not that anally retentive) but in seed trays, plugs and little pots. I am a thorough and evangelical convert to the technique of raising vegetable seedlings in a protected environment.

feb   mar   apr   may   jun   jul   aug   sep   oct   nov   dec

The principle is simple. Seedlings are nurtured through the unreliable early spring weather, its plunging temperatures and harsh winds, and protected against the ravenous slug in the cosy environment of a polytunnel, greenhouse or even a windowsill. From the beginning of March, earlier in some cases, individual seeds of almost any vegetable can be planted in a small, moist plug or pot of compost, where they will begin life without competition or threat. By the time they are planted out – usually directly into the final growing site – they are sturdy enough to withstand an April hailstorm, and big enough to sacrifice a leaf or two to a hungry slug without being fatally injured.

Not everyone approves of plug gardening. Traditionalists argue that plug-raised seedlings are not as hardy as ones sown direct that have had to run the gauntlet of early spring's natural hazards. No doubt there's some truth in this. To minimise the risks it is vital that your seedlings are 'hardened off' before transplanting. Essentially, this means giving them a part-time taste of the wind and weather going on outside their cosy world before the rude awakening of permanent relocation. The standard practice is to place your trays of plugs outside in the morning, then back inside in the evening, for five to seven days before transplanting them. I like to enhance this with short 'sneak previews' of the hardening-off experience earlier in the life of my seedlings. On cold but sunny mornings in March, I'll open the polytunnel at both ends and let the chilly wind blow through. I close it again in time for the afternoon sun to warm up the shivering seedlings before bedtime. I guess it's the same principle as the early-morning cold shower much favoured as a character-forming exercise for schoolboys in bygone days. Not that I approve of that, of course . . .

The consensus, I think it's fair to say, is that plug-starting your seedlings is a particularly effective method for the organic gardener, who has chosen to forsake other, arguably more artificial, leg-ups for young plants, such as chemical fertilisers and pesticides. My own perspective is that it also works admirably well within the raised-bed system of vegetable gardening – of which more in the next chapter.

Ultimately the proof of the pudding is in the eating – literally. Just look at the sheer abundance of my vegetable garden in July (pages 136–7). Practically everything in it was planted in March, in plugs and seed trays in the polytunnel. Truly, the plastic is fantastic.

Ten ways to enjoy purple sprouting broccoli

I dedicate more and more ground to purple sprouting broccoli each year. I just can't get enough of the stuff. This year I have both early and late varieties and they look all set for a bumper crop. I love it because it is such a generous vegetable: sweet and succulent, bursting with good things like a spring tonic, and it keeps on coming.

The fresher it is, the less cooking it needs. My just-picked stems get no more than 3 minutes' steam-boiling (i.e. in a pan with about a centimetre of lightly salted boiling water). Shop-bought PSB, two or three days old, needs about 5–6 minutes to help bring out the sweetness, but no longer or it will be too soft. Some grocers now keep it in bundles with the cut stems in a tray of fresh water, which certainly seems to help. If it looks very tired and floppy, I simply wouldn't buy it.

As I'm eating PSB two or three times a week from late March to early May, I have tried a fair number of accompaniments – enough to compile a pretty worthwhile 'top ten'. Unless otherwise specified, the broccoli is simply steamed and piled on to a warm dish, to be eaten by hand, dipped into whatever concoction happens to be the daily special.

To serve 4 as a starter in each case; use about 500–600g steamed purple sprouting broccoli

Plain melted butter

Melt 125g butter and season with just a few twists of black pepper.

Anchovy and lemon butter

Sweat half a dozen anchovies in 125g butter, stirring well so they more or less dissolve. Add a few twists of black pepper and a generous squeeze of lemon juice.

Cheaty hollandaise

Melt 150g butter and whisk it, a little at a time, into an egg yolk; you should get a loose, mayonnaise-type consistency. Whisk in a good squeeze of lemon juice and season with salt

feb   mar   apr   may   jun   jul   aug   sep   oct   nov   dec

and pepper. This is not a very stable hollandaise but it will hold long enough for you to munch a pile of broccoli – and even if it starts to split it's still quite palatable. Serve warm.

Scrambled eggs (and anchovy)

Make scrambled eggs by melting 50g butter in a small pan and adding 4 eggs that have been lightly beaten with 1 tablespoon cream and seasoned with salt and pepper. Stir regularly but not constantly over a low heat, until very loosely scrambled. Taste and adjust the seasoning. If you like, stir in a dozen anchovy fillets, roughly chopped, before serving.

Tonnata

Grate or crush a clove of garlic and place in a food processor with a 200g tin of tuna, including its oil. Process on pulse, adding the juice of ½ lemon and a good trickle of best olive oil until you have a thick but almost pourable consistency. Stir in 1 heaped teaspoon roughly chopped capers – if you like capers. Taste and adjust the seasoning, adding more lemon juice if necessary. Serve cold as a dip for the hot broccoli.

Anchovy and caper mayonnaise

See the recipe on page 109.

Warm potted shrimp butter

Take a pot of best-quality potted shrimps and roughly chop the shrimps. Then heat them in a small pan with the seasoned butter from the pot. Add a little extra butter (say, 50g) and a good pinch of cayenne pepper. Cook very gently for a couple of minutes to marry the flavours. Serve warm.

Chorizo

Finely chop about 125g spicy chorizo and fry gently in 2 tablespoons olive oil for 4–5 minutes. Add a pinch of cayenne, hot paprika or chilli flakes if you like the heat. Take off the hob and melt a good (50g) knob of butter in the pan. Pour the mixture over the PSB in a warmed bowl and toss well. This one may need a knife and fork.

Rarebit dip

Make the beery, cheesy sauce for the Welsh rarebit on page 50, but without the leeks. Don't grill it on toast but serve it as a fondue-type dip for PSB. Outstanding.

Pasta supper

Chop up about 500g PSB into smaller, forkable pieces. Steam as usual until *al dente*. Cook 250g penne in plenty of boiling salted water until tender. Chop a large clove of garlic and fry it gently in 3 tablespoons olive oil for a couple of minutes, without letting it colour. Add a tin of anchovies, drained and chopped, and a tin of tuna, drained and flaked. Shake together in the pan until well mixed, then toss with the just-cooked PSB and the just-drained pasta. Season with black pepper and serve at once.

Lightly salted relatives of cod in beer batter

The chip shop has made battered cod one of the nation's favourite dishes. And personally I think that's a reason for pride. At its best, it is a sensational dish. The question, of course, is can chip-shop perfection be achieved in the privacy of your own home? The answer, I'm delighted to say, is yes.

Cod is the king of fish for battering (except in the north-east, where haddock reigns supreme). But at a time when cod stocks are alarmingly low, it's as well to be aware of some superb, and cheaper, alternatives. March is the month when good catches of large pollack are landed in Dorset. Long regarded as a poor relation (it is a member of the cod family), pollack is nevertheless an important commercial fish, as vast quantities are used to make those weird fish-flavoured sticks. It deserves a better fate – and is starting to get one, as much of what is labelled as smoked haddock is in fact actually smoked pollack. But it has

feb   mar   apr   may   jun   jul   aug   sep   oct   nov   dec

merit as a fresh fish, too (the French love it), and it's likely to appear more and more often on the wet-fish slab. Ask your local fishmonger about it.

Pollack is well worth battering. And by lightly salting it first, you can counter the slight wetness of its flesh and improve the texture of the finished dish. In fact, this is a good strategy for cod too, but does wonders for all its poor relations, with whom we are likely to become increasingly familiar. Besides pollack, look out for, and be ready to embrace, whiting, ling, coley and even the much-derided pouting. They'll all respond superbly to this treatment.

To serve 4 – 6

First prepare the batter. Sift 200g plain flour into a large bowl with a few twists of black pepper and a pinch of salt. Mix in 2 tablespoons olive or groundnut oil, then beat in, a little at a time, 250ml good beer – anything really, including stout, but preferably not cheap lager. Leave this thick, pasty batter to rest while you prepare the fish.

Sprinkle a thin, even layer of flaky or coarse salt on a board. Take 4–6 fillets of pollack or other good white fish, up to 250g in weight, and lay them skin-side down on the salted board (or skin them first, if you prefer). Sprinkle another thin layer of salt over the fillets. Leave for just 15 minutes, then rinse the salt off under cold running water and immediately pat the fish dry with kitchen paper. Season with a few twists of black pepper and leave for another 10 minutes to settle.

In a large, heavy saucepan or a deep-fat fryer, heat a good 10cm depth of oil (groundnut is my choice) to about 160°C on a kitchen thermometer, or so that a piece of bread turns deep golden brown in it in 2–3 minutes.

Whisk 2 egg whites until they form soft peaks. Loosen the batter a little with a couple more tablespoons of beer, then quickly fold in the egg whites. Dip a fish portion in the batter so it is completely coated, then lower carefully into the hot oil. Deep-fry for about 4–5 minutes, turning once, until golden brown, then remove carefully with a large deep-frying basket. Place on a warmed dish lined with several layers of kitchen paper and leave in a warm place, or put in a low oven, while you attend to the next portion.

Oddly enough, I don't always feel the need for chips with my battered fish, but I do love a side order of mushy peas and tartare sauce. See my recipes over the page.

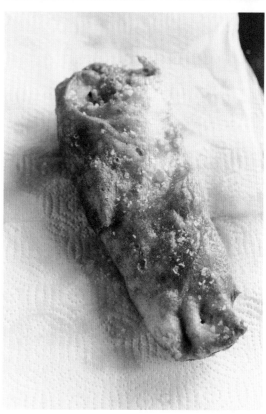

My mushy peas

I love mushy peas with battered fish. This version is a kind of cross between the fresh pea purée on page 164 and the split pea purée I serve with my goose leg confit (page 240). The combination of mealy dried peas and sweet fresh or frozen ones is pea heaven.

To serve 4 – 6

Soak **250g dried green split peas** in cold water overnight, if you have time. Drain well, then boil in plenty of lightly salted water (with **an onion** and **a carrot**, if you like) until completely tender. This may take up to an hour — test by removing a couple of peas and crushing them between finger and thumb. Add to the same pan about **250g frozen or fresh peas**. Bring back to the boil and simmer for 4–6 minutes until these, too, are completely tender. Drain the peas, reserving some of the cooking liquid but discarding the onion and carrot, if used, and place in a food processor with about **50g soft butter**. Pulse to a coarse purée, adding a little of the cooking liquid if you want to loosen it. Taste and adjust the seasoning. Reheat and serve piping hot.

— —

A dill tartare sauce

Bought versions of tartare sauce are invariably disappointing — all vinegar and no herbs. But it's easy to knock up at home. This is the version I like to make for my battered fish. If I plant dill in the polytunnel in early February, I should have a first pick by the middle of March.

Mix a generous heaped tablespoon of **mayonnaise** (preferably home-made) with an equal quantity of **crème fraîche**. Stir in a finely chopped **hard-boiled egg**, 1 tablespoon finely chopped **gherkins or small dill pickled cucumber**, 1 tablespoon chopped **fresh dill**, ¼ tablespoon **English mustard** and a pinch each of **salt** and **pepper**. Done.

Nettle (and sorrel) risotto

Purple sprouting broccoli may be the only green vegetable in the garden, but in the hedgerow all kinds of edible greens are starting to show. In particular, the fresh young shoots of nettles should not be overlooked. They make a great soup, which I described in *The River Cottage Cookbook*, and also a very fine risotto. It's even better if you combine the nettles with wild or cultivated sorrel.

To serve 2 as a main course, 4 as a starter

Wearing stout rubber gloves and thick socks, pick a generous colander-full of young nettles – the top 4 or 6 leaves of each young plant. Pick as many wild sorrel leaves as you can – up to half the quantity of nettles. Or use cultivated sorrel from the garden.

Rinse the leaves thoroughly and pick them over, discarding grass, bugs etc and separating the sorrel from the nettles. Bring a large pan of well-salted water to boiling point and throw in the nettle tops, but not the sorrel. Bring back to the boil and blanch for a couple of minutes, then drain, saving the liquid. Squeeze well in a colander or sieve to extract as much water as possible (you could make this into a strong nettle tea, as described on page 63 – a great tonic for the blood). Finely chop the squeezed nettle leaves. Finely chop the sorrel too, and set aside.

Heat about 900ml vegetable or chicken stock till almost boiling and then leave over a very low heat. In a separate heavy-based saucepan, sweat an onion, finely chopped, in about 50g butter until soft and translucent but not browned. Add 175g Arborio rice and mix well for a few seconds to coat the grains with oil, then pour in a third of the stock and bring to a gentle simmer. Cook, stirring, until almost all the stock has been absorbed. Add the chopped nettles and a little more stock.

From then on, add more stock a little at a time until all the liquid has been absorbed and the rice is nicely *al dente*. You may not need all the stock, but the texture should be loose and creamy. Now stir in the finely shredded sorrel leaves. Check and adjust the seasoning.

Stir another knob of butter and a good 50g grated Parmesan into the risotto. Serve straight away, with more Parmesan and the grater at the table.

feb   mar   apr   may   jun   jul   aug   sep   oct   nov   dec

Crispy seaweed greens

The delicious and ubiquitous oriental dish known as crispy seaweed isn't really seaweed at all. Instead it's made with any of a number of leafy greens. I spent an afternoon experimenting with kale, cabbage and spring greens and found that all of them lent themselves to this treatment. You can even use Brussels tops and the leaves of purple sprouting broccoli. But spring and winter greens are probably the best.

Traditionally, this dish is an aphrodisiac!

To serve 4

Take about **250g spring greens** (or any of the leaves mentioned above). Trim out the coarse central stems, then wash and pat dry the leaves. Tightly roll up a bunch of the leaves like a fat cigar (on your inner thigh, if you like). Then shred the leaves as finely as you possibly can – maximum 2mm per shred!

Heat at least 5cm of **sunflower or groundnut oil** in a deep heavy saucepan or deep-fat fryer, until a small piece of bread dropped into the oil will turn golden brown in about 30 seconds.

Take a small handful of shredded greens and drop them in the hot oil. Remove with a draining basket after just 15–30 seconds, by which time they should be completely crisp. If they're not, then the oil needs to be hotter.

Continue to fry in small batches, draining each quickly on kitchen paper and piling them up like a bird's nest on a warm plate. Traditionally, crispy seaweed is served with a sprinkling of grated **dried scallop**, which you can find at most oriental supermarkets. But a scattering of **toasted sesame seeds** and a good shake of **soy sauce** make an excellent alternative.

Eat straight away, with chopsticks.

feb   mar   apr   may   jun   jul   aug   sep   oct   nov   dec

Primrose and champagne jelly

This is an Edwardian dish, which I made, somewhat sceptically I have to admit, for the television series, *Treats from the Edwardian Country House*. It turned out to be a delicious, adult concoction. It's only fair to say that the primroses don't really contribute to the flavour of this jelly, which is really all about the champagne and citrus fruits. Still, the flowers make for a stunning visual treat, and seem to me to stimulate sensations of sap rising, so why not indulge? You should end up with the kind of quivering seasonal sculpture you see on pages 60–61.

Pick primroses from your garden (or someone else's!) but not from the wild, which is technically illegal.

To serve 6 – 8

Put 7 gelatine leaves to soak in a shallow dish of water for 5 minutes (or follow the packet instructions for setting 1 litre of liquid). Meanwhile, in a large saucepan, put 125g caster sugar, two-thirds of a bottle (500ml) champagne or dry sparkling wine, a 175ml glass of sherry, 250ml water and the grated zest and juice of 1 orange and 1 lemon. Stir over a low heat until the sugar has dissolved. Add the soaked gelatine and stir to dissolve that too. Lightly whisk 2 egg whites, crush the shells and add the whites and shells to the pan. Stir occasionally until the liquid is very frothy and comes almost to the boil. Remove from the heat and strain through a thoroughly wetted cotton cloth or jelly bag into a bowl. (The egg white and shell treatment is not essential but it will make the jelly crystal clear.)

Pour about a quarter of the jelly into a suitably dashing jelly mould, about 1 litre in capacity. Place in the fridge until lightly set. Arrange a ring of primrose flowers, open petals down, on the surface of the jelly, pressing lightly so they stick to the tacky surface. Carefully pour over the next quarter of the unset jelly and put the mould back into the fridge. Continue in this way, creating 2 or 3 rings of primroses set into the jelly.

To unmould the jelly, dip the mould briefly in hot water and use the tip of your finger to judge when the jelly is coming away from the sides. Place your chosen serving dish over the top, flip it over with a little shake and lift off the mould. Easier said than done, I know.

You could serve the jelly with a splash of freshly popped champagne poured over the top.

Hot cross buns

I have always loved hot cross buns and decided to teach myself how to make them this year. I tried various recipes and this one, adapted from *The Sunday Times* cookery writer of the Sixties and Seventies, Margaret Costa, was by far the best. The texture is light and very bunny, with no residual taste of yeast.

To make 16 buns

Sift **500g plain flour**, in 2 lots of 250g, into 2 mixing bowls. Mix **125ml cold milk** with 125ml boiling water and a good pinch of **sugar** to give a lukewarm milk-and-water mix and add 2 level teaspoons (about 10g) **dried yeast**. When the surface is frothy and the yeast well activated, add the liquid to one bowl of flour and mix well to get a smooth but wet and sticky batter. Leave this wet batter, covered, in a warm place for about 45 minutes. It should rise to almost double in volume. Meanwhile, mix the remaining portion of flour with ½ teaspoon fine **salt**, 1–2 teaspoons **ground mixed spice** (according to your taste), **50g caster sugar**, **125g raisins** (or currants or sultanas, if you prefer) and 1 teaspoon each of **grated orange and lemon zest**.

Add this dry mix to the risen batter, along with **50g melted butter** and **½ beaten egg**. Mix thoroughly with a wooden spoon, then knead it in the bowl with well-floured hands to get a dough that is on the sticky side but just manageable. Leave to rise again for about an hour, until doubled in size.

Turn the risen dough out on to a well-floured surface and, without kneading again, cut it into 2, then 4, then 8, then 16 pieces. With floured hands, gently pat your 16 pieces into nice, round bun shapes. Space them evenly on a greased and lightly floured baking tray.

To make the crosses you can use narrow ribbons of **pastry, or a simple flour and water dough**. Take 2 finger-long strips, wet one side of each and stick them over the bun in a cross. Leave for a final rise for just 15–20 minutes, then brush with a little **beaten egg** and bake in the centre of a moderately hot oven (200°C/Gas Mark 6) for 15 minutes.

Split and butter the buns when still warm and, I would say, eat without any honey or jam. They'll keep for 2 or 3 days – reheat in a hot oven for 4–5 minutes, or split and toast.

Simnel cake

This is the traditional Easter cake, which I have adapted to make it a little fresher and zestier. I baked it in the Easter television programme of River Cottage Forever and have since been inundated with requests for the recipe. Here, finally, it is.

First make a big ball of marzipan. In a large mixing bowl combine 350g ground almonds with 250g icing sugar. Stir in 1 scant tablespoon lemon juice, then add 3 beaten egg yolks, a little at a time, and maybe not all of it, working the mix with your hands to get a stiff paste that doesn't crack when kneaded. Wrap in clingfilm and set aside.

To make the cake, sift 250g plain flour with ½ teaspoon salt, 2 level teaspoons baking powder and 1 level teaspoon ground mixed spice. Cream 200g soft unsalted butter with 200g light brown sugar until light and airy. Beat in 3 eggs, one at a time, with a tablespoon of the sifted flour mix going in after each egg. Fold in the remaining flour in 2 or 3 batches, alternately with the juice of 1 lemon and ½ orange. Then fold in 200g each of currants, raisins and sultanas, 125g chopped mixed candied peel (optional) and the finely grated zest of 1 orange and 1 lemon. Mix to a thoroughly well blended batter.

Pile half the mixture into a lined and greased high-sided 20cm cake tin, then level the top. Make a ball of a little less than half the marzipan and press or roll it out to a circle that fits snugly in the tin. Lay this over the cake mixture, then spread the second half of the mixture on top. Bake in the centre of a fairly low oven (150°C/Gas Mark 2) for 2–2½ hours, until the top is golden brown and a knife blade pushed into the centre (but not as far as the marzipan, which will smear it) comes out clean.

Remove from the oven and leave to cool in the tin. Turn out of the tin and brush the top with a little melted jam. Roll out the remaining marzipan into a neat circle and lay it over the top of the cake. Flash under a hot grill to get a lightly toasted surface, then leave to cool again.

Traditionally the cake is decorated with 11 balls of marzipan, representing the 12 apostles minus Judas, so set some marzipan aside if you want to do this. Primrose flowers (from the garden, not wild) dipped in lightly beaten egg white, then caster sugar, and left to harden in an airing cupboard make another pretty, edible and seasonal flourish.

feb   mar   apr   may   jun   jul   aug   sep   oct   nov   dec

APRIL _____

I don't think April is the cruellest month – I'd give that gong to February. But April can certainly give you grief as well as goodness. To get the best out of it, it helps to have a mildly masochistic temperament – but then all farmers and gardeners need that.

The gardening pendulum swings from chore to pleasure, depending not just on the task in hand but also on the weather's constant pranking. With schizophrenic temperatures that plunge one from shirtsleeves into double jumpers in a matter of minutes, it may still be buttered crumpets at teatime after a day of April gardening. Then one evening the sun, now up until after eight, may have enough residual warmth to justify drinks on the lawn. With a bit of luck that'll be my first rhubarb Bellini of the year (page 100).

A month for growing rather than reaping, April may hold more tangible pleasures for the vegetable gardener than for the cook – so with a bit of luck they are one and the same. For me, it's the time to be admiring and nurturing my seedlings, plug-planted from early March (see page 64), while lovingly attending to the soil in which they are going to be planted out.

There's no denying that soil preparation, aka digging, requires a certain amount of graft. But the back-straining toil is considerably reduced by the raised bed system. The objective is low-maintenance beds that are easy to weed and require less deep digging less often. The key to this is that whether you are weeding, planting, digging or harvesting your crop, the beds can be tended from the surrounding path without any need to tread on and compress the soil of the bed itself. If you can avoid soil compacting for the whole growing season, and keep the bed relatively weed-free, then the only digging necessary in preparation for the next season is that required to mix in a hefty dose of well-rotted compost or animal muck.

The raised bed system is really an extensive form of container gardening, with the 'containers' in question being larger and shallower – and, of course, permanently sited. The ideal width of the beds is 80–120cm. Anything from 50–120cm deep is suitable. The poorer the soil, the more reason to make a deeper raised bed – you will want to add considerable amounts of fresh organic material each season. And they can be anything from 2–5 metres long, with 3–4 metres being a good practical and aesthetic proportion.

Although stone, bricks and breeze blocks can be used to make permanent raised beds, they will prove both expensive and inflexible. The preferred material for constructing the edges is therefore wood in various forms: railway sleepers, old telegraph poles, pairs of fence poles lashed together and laid down lengthways or, simplest and cheapest of all (and my choice), scaffolder's duckboards. These should be nailed to 5cm square posts, or 10cm diameter half-round posts, which have been hammered as deep as possible (at least 50cm) into the ground. The heavier edges, such as railway sleepers, can just be pegged into place with the half-rounds. Beware of heavily creosoted wood, as this may contaminate the soil on contact (it's something to watch out for with those railway sleepers).

If DIY is not your forte, or you don't want to commit to anything as permanent as these structures, there is a very practical halfway house to the raised bed, which I highly recommend. The 'straw path' system can be laid out on any piece of cultivated ground. Instead of creating containing edges for your beds, simply define the beds (in recommended units of 1 x 4 metres) by laying out a network of thick straw paths, 40–50cm wide, between them. At first the straw will be piled up above the level of the beds but as you use it as a path it will become increasingly compacted, eventually falling below the level of the beds. The compacted straw is a very effective barrier to any grass and weeds trying to come through.

Once the paths are in place, the same principle as for raised beds is applied: the beds are tended and maintained from the paths without the gardener ever treading on the soil. The paths are even rather comfortable to kneel on when weeding. Another practical bonus is that any weeds removed from the beds can simply be thrown on the paths, where they will be trodden down and destroyed, eventually to be composted along with the straw.

You can maintain a straw path system for two or even three seasons, removing all the compacted straw to the compost heap once a year and replacing it, and adding plenty of muck

feb   mar   apr   may   jun   jul   aug   sep   oct   nov   dec

or compost to the beds in the autumn. But after three seasons it's best to dig over the entire patch, manure it well, and reconfigure your straw paths in new orientations.

I'm now cultivating a combination of raised beds and a network of straw-pathed beds – you can see the layout (and the effectiveness!) in the July picture on pages 136–7. Now, every April, a couple of hours on each bed generally does the job. The autumn-laid compost or well-rotted manure is dug in. Alternatively, the compost or manure I never quite got round to spreading in the autumn goes on now, and is dug in straight away, as thoroughly as possible. This isn't an ideal scenario, if you're trying to create a fine tilth for sowing seeds. But, for 'plug gardening', where sturdy seedlings go straight into the beds, it's fine.

There's stuff to take out of the beds as well as put in. In my flinty Dorset soil, bucketloads of stones come to the surface, even if last year I thought I'd cleared out the lot of them. Weed roots and weed seedlings are removed, too – with the satisfaction, I imagine, of a good Sunday-school session: wickedness banished before it has a chance to take hold of young souls and corrupt them.

The one thing I will sow directly this month – which will have no trouble at all with a rough-and-ready raised bed, provided it's very muck rich – is potatoes. Many keen gardeners will have got their first spuds in by the end of March. But my preferred varieties – waxy Pink Fir Apples and creamy, oval La Rattes and Charlottes – are maincrop types, even though they are eaten as 'new'. They'll be happier going in with a little April warmth to see them right. Between the rows of spuds, the first of successive radish sowings will go in too. They might like a finer tilth than they'll get among the spuds, but they'll sort themselves out. I ring the changes with varieties, as I have yet to come across a dull radish, but the round Sparkler and the long, white-tipped French Breakfast have been recent favourites. I'll sow fortnightly until perhaps late May, when the thriving potato plants will cast too much shade over them.

We should at least be reaping in the field. The ram goes in to 'tup' my ewes on Guy Fawkes' Day, which is traditional for those who wish to lamb their flock in spring. It means lambs can be expected from April Fool's Day onwards. It also means that, with a bit of luck, you can leave all but your first-lamb ewes out of doors to deliver unassisted. There may be casualties, and this can seem tough to some. But over time it means you are selecting ewes who are good independent birthers. It's not the way of the commercial herds but it suits me.

Seedling salad

I sow my first vegetables of the year, mostly salads, in mid- or late February. The seeds go into plugs and seed trays in the polytunnel, which, however harsh the weather, is pretty much frost proof. A month or so later, some are ready for planting out, either in the polytunnel bed or, with frost-proof seedlings such as peas and beans, outside (after hardening off).

Inevitably I sow far more than I need – especially of the lettuces and other leafy greens. But these seedlings may have a good 4 or 5 inches of growth already – far too much edible leaf to waste. So I harvest them to make a symbolic 'first salad' of the year. In fact, with good polytunnel management, I may still be cropping the winter salad greens at the same time as these spring seedlings are ready. But by this time the winter lettuces – tatsoi, mizuna, rocket and various chicories – are coarse, and their pungent, bitter flavours are beginning to pall. By contrast the tiny spring leaves, auguring a whole summer of salads to come, are so delicate, tender and sweet that even if they offer only a scant plate for the three of us to share, the exercise is worthwhile.

My seedling salad will include a variety of **tiny lettuces, both Cos and butterhead types.** The other thing I always like to use is a few **pea shoots.** The young tips, with 3 or 4 leaves attached, can be plucked without harming the rest of the seedling, which will rapidly grow back. They have a wonderful leguminous taste that is delicious with a little light olive oil and lemon dressing. I like pea shoots in a salad so much that I now dedicate a tub in the polytunnel to peas for 'salad only' purposes, plucking them mercilessly and even re-sowing in midsummer and early autumn. You'll already see pea shoots in restaurants that take their salads seriously. I have a hunch they'll be coming to a supermarket near you soon.

I also like to pinch a few **baby spinach leaves** and sometimes I might include, for a little bite, some **chives** in half-finger lengths, or a few tiny new **rocket leaves** – taken from a direct February sowing (rocket is so feisty and prolific that there's no need to bother with plugs), never the coarse winter leftovers.

The leaves should be lightly washed and gently dried – shake them in a tea towel rather than risk bruising them in a salad spinner. The dressing must be simple and unobtrusive –

feb   mar   apr   may   jun   jul   aug   sep   oct   nov   dec

i.e. no mustard or garlic. Try a tablespoon of good olive oil mixed with just a couple of teaspoons of lemon juice or good vinegar, plus a pinch of sugar, salt and pepper.

Actually, this recipe gets another seasonal hit about seven months later in September/October. Just as the tomatoes come out of the polytunnel, the seedlings of the aforementioned winter salads, again planted in plugs a month or so before, go in. There are the usual surplus seedlings, but this time of the pungent and powerful chicories and oriental greens. So it's a whole different salad, one that marks a big change in the season and braces one for the winter to come.

- -

Warm potato and wilted sorrel salad

If you didn't see any wild sorrel peeping through in March it should certainly be around by April. And if you grow the cultivated variety in your garden, you'll know that, having overwintered it, you can expect the first decent crop around now. The first Jersey Royals should be in the shops by the end of the month too. Try this recipe with them, and revisit it later in the year when the delectable waxy potato varieties, La Ratte, Epicure and Pink Fir Apple, become available. This is close to being the easiest recipe in the whole book, and it is also one of my favourites. I like to serve it as a dish on its own, or as a side dish with simply cooked fish — especially an early trout or salmon.

To serve 4 as a starter

Scrub about 500g new potatoes, such as Jersey Royals, and boil them in well-salted water until just tender. Jersey Royals in particular lose much of their charm if overboiled, so be vigilant and taste a small potato after just 7 minutes or so; 8–10 minutes is often long enough.

While the potatoes are cooking, strip the central veins out of 2 or 3 good fistfuls of sorrel (wild or cultivated). Wash well and shred into ribbons about 1cm wide.

As soon as the potatoes are ready, drain them and put in a bowl with a large knob (about 50g) butter and a trickle of olive oil. Throw the shredded sorrel into the bowl and toss well. Leave for a minute, so the heat of the potatoes wilts the sorrel, then toss again. Rest for another minute, then season with salt and pepper and serve at once.

Eel with chilli, ginger and garlic

I am sometimes asked why I bother to include recipes like this in my books. People say, 'Do you really think that someone's going to bother to go looking for a pike/eel/squirrel/pig's trotter?' The answer is, I don't suppose that vast numbers do but I know, because they write and tell me, that some have. And that's all the justification I need. If we let these good things simply fall off our cultural menu, then the loss would be a tragedy.

In fact, for anyone who has a little bit of a psychological problem with eels – could be Freudian, could be Jungian – this is the dish to banish the demons and help you develop a healthy love for one of the most delicious and versatile fishes. If you are wondering where you might get hold of a nice fresh eel, then just try and think of anyone you know who regularly goes coarse fishing. They're sure to catch a few eels in the course of their sport, and might be willing to kill and keep one for you. Failing that, there is still a market in eels, thanks largely to their popularity in the Chinese restaurant trade. So in theory, any good fishmonger should be able to order one or two from his wholesaler.

To serve 4 as a starter

Take a good-sized eel of 400g upwards and gut and skin it. Skinning is best done by making a shallow incision through the skin of the eel in a circle round the base of the head. Then use a pair of pliers or a dry cotton cloth to get a grip on the skin and peel it off in one tubular piece, like a stocking. Take your sharpest knife and fillet the eel by running the knife as close

as you can to the eel's backbone – it's actually quite easy. Cut the fillets on the bias into 3–4cm strips. Finely chop a couple of garlic cloves, a small, fairly hot red chilli (or use dried chilli flakes) and a thumb-top-sized nugget of peeled fresh ginger root. Toss the eel pieces with these ingredients and a few twists of black pepper and leave for at least 10 minutes, better an hour, for the flavours to marry and mingle.

Heat some oil for deep-frying (my preference is groundnut oil) in a large pan or deep-fat fryer until a piece of bread dropped in it turns golden brown in about a minute. Season 50g plain flour (or, better still, cornflour) with a good sprinkling of salt. Toss half a dozen pieces of the marinated eel, with the flecks of garlic, chilli and ginger still sticking to them, in the seasoned flour, then lower carefully into the hot oil. Deep-fry for 2–3 minutes, until golden brown and crisp. Drain on kitchen paper as you fry the next batch.

Eat piping hot, with chopsticks. You can make a very nice dipping sauce by mixing 3 parts soy sauce with 1 part rice vinegar and stirring in a finely sliced spring onion. Alternatively, the plum dipping sauce on page 189 makes a superb accompaniment.

- -

Wood pigeon with red wine and raisins

Wood pigeons are resourceful and effective winter feeders, and in all but the most severe winters (a distant memory these days) they keep their condition pretty well over the cold months. Nonetheless, the arrival of spring seedlings, peas and beans, and rape in particular, is a great resource for them, and they should be in good nick by the end of the month – for eating as well as breeding.

This recipe is based on a lovely old-fashioned pigeon stew, but I've changed the emphasis so that the breasts can be flash-fried and served rare, while the carcasses go to make a wonderful stock that can be reduced to make an intense, fruity sauce. It's quite a cheffy dish, I admit, but it isn't hard, and sometimes it's fun to cook like this.

To serve 4

Slice the breasts off 4 oven-ready pigeons, as close to the bone as you can. Marinate these, if you like, in 1 tablespoon olive oil, with ½ finely sliced onion, a few sprigs of fresh thyme (or ½ teaspoon of dried) and a few twists of black pepper.

Cut 2 large carrots into chunks and 2 onions in half. Brush the breastless pigeon carcasses and the vegetables with olive oil and place them in a roasting tin. Roast in a moderately hot oven (200°C/Gas Mark 6) for about half an hour, until well browned, then transfer to a stockpot. Deglaze the still-hot roasting tin by pouring in a glass of red wine and scraping up all the burnt bits, then add these juices to the pot. Add a couple of bay leaves and enough water just to cover the carcasses. Bring to the boil and simmer very gently for at least 2 hours, 3 or 4 if you like, to give a well-flavoured stock.

Meanwhile, put 2 tablespoons raisins in a small pan, cover with a glass of good red wine and bring to the boil. Remove from the heat immediately, cover and leave to macerate.

Strain the stock through a sieve and then through muslin or a cotton cloth. Put it in a clean pan and boil hard until reduced to a scant 250ml. Strain in the wine from the raisins and continue to reduce till you have just a few tablespoonfuls of intense gravy. Only now should you season the sauce (any earlier and it would become unpalatably salty as it reduces). Then add the raisins and simmer gently for a couple of minutes to plump them up.

Take the pigeon breasts from the marinade and wipe clean. Heat a little dripping or oil in a heavy frying pan until fairly hot. Flash-fry the breasts in the pan, turning occasionally, and seasoning, until they are nicely browned – no longer than 4 minutes in all, if you like your meat rare, 5–6 minutes for medium, 7–8 if you want to spoil it!

Leave the pigeon breasts to rest on a wooden board for 10 minutes. Then slice each one on the bias into 3 or 4 thick slices, showing the nice pink meat in the middle. Arrange 2 sliced breasts on each of 4 warmed plates and spoon over the sauce, with plenty of raisins over the breasts. Serve with creamy mashed potatoes and lightly steamed, buttered greens.

feb   mar   apr   may   jun   jul   aug   sep   oct   nov   dec

Sorrel soup

We're lucky enough to have a ready supply of wild sorrel growing in the fields near where we live. But as it tends to get coarse and go to seed by early June, I also grow the cultivated variety in the garden. This stays tender and usable as long as you keep picking it, and cut off any flower buds as soon as they appear.

I'm giving sorrel a second outing in this chapter because it really deserves more attention, and this soup is quite superb. The poached egg finish turns a soup into a supper.

To serve 2

Pick a few good handfuls of sorrel, about 75–100g in all, wash well and trim off any particularly coarse stalks.

Melt a knob of butter in a saucepan over a low heat and add 1 onion, finely chopped, 1 large or 2 medium leeks, finely sliced, and 1 large or 2 medium carrots, chopped. Sweat gently for about 5 minutes, so the vegetables are slightly softened but not coloured. Add about 600ml good chicken or vegetable stock and 2 tablespoons long grain rice, well rinsed. Bring to the boil and simmer until the rice is completely tender.

Ladle the soup into a blender, adding the raw sorrel, another knob of butter and 1 tablespoon double cream. Blend until completely smooth (depending on the capacity of your blender, you may have to do this in two batches). Return the soup to the pan, reheat thoroughly without boiling and adjust the seasoning with salt and pepper.

To finish: The perfect poached egg

Poach the eggs one at a time. Break each egg (which should be at room temperature) into a cup, being careful not to break the yolk. Bring a small pan of lightly salted water to the boil. When it is boiling rapidly, stir fast with a large spoon to create a vortex. Pour the egg into the centre of the vortex, place the lid on the pan and turn off the heat. Leave for exactly 2 minutes.

Serve the soup in a warmed bowl with the drained poached egg in the centre and an extra little blob of cream beside it.

Home-made ricotta

Traditionally the quality of milk improves in April, as the dairy herds come out of their winter housing and graze on the new growth of grass – which is richer than at any other time of year. You may taste the difference on your breakfast cereals.

It's a good time to do a very simple bit of cheese-making – and this is the easiest cheese you'll ever make. The result isn't strictly speaking ricotta but it is remarkably similar in both taste and texture. And it's superbly versatile, with all kinds of sweet and savoury uses.

Provided you're not in a risk group for food poisoning, such as pregnant women or the very old or very young (I have to say this, by the way), then it will be even more delicious if you make it with unpasteurised milk, which gives it a fuller, more cow-y flavour.

Scald a large saucepan with a kettle of boiling water to sterilise it. Then add 2 litres fresh whole milk (unpasteurised if you can get it) and a pinch of salt. Heat gently to blood temperature (use the thermometer from the medicine cabinet if you're in any doubt) and remove at once from the heat. Add 4 teaspoons rennet (which you can buy in chemist's, health-food shops and some supermarkets) and stir well in. Leave for about 15 minutes, while the milk separates into curds (at the top) and whey (at the bottom).

Use a slotted spoon or small sieve to skim off the curds, in as large pieces as possible, placing them in a colander lined with a large square of double-layered muslin. When you've skimmed off almost all the curds, tie up the corners of the muslin and hang the cheese to drip above a sink or bucket. Leave for about 3 hours, then unwrap the cheese, place in a pudding basin, cover and store in the fridge.

The cheese you now have is sweet, soft and curdy – very much like ricotta. Keep it covered, in a bowl in the fridge, and it will stay fresh and 'sweet' for 2–3 days. After that, the flavour will gradually turn more tangy and cheesy – still good to eat, but perhaps more suited to cooking and savoury applications. Use it up within a week.

You can use it in any recipe that calls for ricotta, including pasta stuffings and various Italian cakes and savouries. But if you want to enjoy it for its own sake, try a few of the following concoctions, savoury and sweet:

feb   mar   apr   may   jun   jul   aug   sep   oct   nov   dec

SAVOURY

Ricotta and lentil salad

Lay thin slices of cold home-made ricotta over warm Puy lentils, dressed with a little olive oil and lemon juice. Season with salt and pepper and trickle over more olive oil.

Spinach with ricotta and Parmesan

Crumble the home-made ricotta over buttered wilted spinach, then grate some fresh Parmesan over that.

Tagliatelle ricotta carbonara

To serve 4 as a starter, put 250g tagliatelle on to cook in plenty of well-salted boiling water. Fry 125g diced bacon or pancetta in a little olive oil with a finely chopped garlic clove until lightly crisp. Beat 3 eggs with 150ml double cream and 50g grated Parmesan, then season well with salt and pepper. When the pasta is cooked, drain it and return to the hot pan. Toss with the bacon and the Parmesan, egg and cream mixture, so it's lightly cooked by the residual heat of the pan and pasta. Divide between 4 warmed plates. Crumble curds of the home-made ricotta over the hot pasta and eat at once.

Ricotta omelette

Lightly beat 3 eggs with a fork and season with salt and pepper. Heat a knob of butter in a small frying pan and gently cook the eggs, agitating them occasionally with a spatula. While the omelette is still a little runny on the surface, crumble over a couple of handfuls of home-made ricotta, then fold the omelette over it. Leave for a minute or two, then serve up.

SWEET

With lemon and sugar

Spoon a few curds of home-made ricotta into a bowl and sprinkle with caster sugar. Add a squeeze of lemon or orange juice, or both, and eat with a spoon.

Greek yoghurt style

Serve the ricotta with a sliced banana and a trickle of runny honey. Later in the year, do it with strawberries and/or fresh peaches.

On toast

Lay a slice of home-made ricotta on a piece of toast or, better still, French toast (aka eggy bread) and sprinkle with brown sugar and cinnamon.

With rhubarb

Combine the ricotta with a sweetened but still tart compote of stewed rhubarb (see below), mixing roughly so the ricotta stays in small curds.

- -

Rhubarb and custard trifle

April marks the end of the season for forced indoor rhubarb (which begins in mid-December) and the beginning of the season for outdoor cultivated rhubarb. So, two excellent reasons for thinking about rhubarb this month. I hardly need an excuse, as I love the stuff. This is my favourite rhubarb pudding.

To serve 6

Wash, trim and cut into 5cm lengths about 500g rhubarb (forced or outdoor, as available). Put in a pan with 100ml freshly squeezed orange juice and 4 tablespoons sugar. Bring to a simmer and cook gently until the stalks are tender but still hold their shape. Taste the rhubarb; it should be tart, as the sponge and custard will sweeten the trifle. But if it's unpalatably sour, add a little more sugar. Strain off about 200ml of the juice. Transfer the remaining rhubarb to a non-metallic dish. Chill both juice and rhubarb in the fridge.

feb   mar   apr   may   jun   jul   aug   sep   oct   nov   dec

Make a rich custard. Put 250ml double cream and 250ml whole milk in a pan with a split vanilla pod and scald till not quite boiling. Beat 4 large egg yolks with 100g caster sugar and whisk in the hot cream. Return this custard to the pan over a very low heat and stir constantly until it thickens, making a glossy coat on the back of the spoon. Remove from the heat and continue to stir for a minute as it cools. Then strain through a sieve into a bowl and chill. When cold, it should be spoonably thick rather than pourable.

Take (or make) a simple plain sponge cake, such as Victoria or Genoese sponge. Break it into chunks and press lightly into 6 large wine glasses, filling the bottom third. Pour in enough of the chilled rhubarb juice to soak the sponge thoroughly.

Now pile in a generous layer (the next third of the glass) of the chilled, thickened custard. And then top with a layer of the stewed rhubarb. You can, if you like, top with a mound of stiffly whipped cream and a sprinkling of toasted almonds. But I prefer the pure rhubarb and custard version.

- -

Rhubarb cocktails

You may be sceptical but I urge you to try some — all — of these drinks. They are genuinely classy cocktails and the zesty tang of rhubarb makes them uniquely refreshing.

All the cocktails are based on a light rhubarb syrup, poured off from a pan of stewed rhubarb. The rhubarb itself can be used to make a classic fool or crumble.

To serve 6

Wash and cut up 500g rhubarb and put it in a pan with the juice of 2 oranges and 4 tablespoons sugar. Gently stew the rhubarb at a quiet simmer for about 10 minutes, until it is quite tender. Use a sieve to strain off the syrup into a jar. Leave to cool, then put it in the fridge to chill.

The syrup will keep in a sealed jar in the fridge for up to a month.

feb   mar   apr   may   jun   jul   aug   sep   oct   nov   dec

Rhubarb Bellini

My personal favourite, this really gives the classic peach Bellini a run for its money. A great seasonal variation is the plum Bellini, which can be made in exactly the same way, with any good cooking plum, in August and September.

The right ratio of champagne or dry sparkling wine to rhubarb syrup is about 4:1. With this in mind, pour a good slosh of syrup into a flute and top up with chilled champagne or dry sparkling wine. The mix will foam enthusiastically, so let it settle and top up again.

You can use a baby rhubarb stalk dipped in lightly beaten egg white and then caster sugar as a decorative but edible swizzle stick.

Rhubarb vodkatini

If you're sold on the notion of rhubarb cocktails after the Bellini (and I think you will be), and you like a stiffer drink, try pouring 2 parts vodka, 1 part rhubarb syrup and a pinch of ground ginger into a cocktail shaker with ice. Shake and strain into a martini glass. Serve with a short baton of raw rhubarb in the bottom of the glass (instead of the olive).

Rhubarb Mule

For a long summer drink, mix the rhubarb syrup with an equal quantity of vodka, pour over ice in a tall glass, add a few bruised mint leaves and top up with ginger ale.

Rhubarb Margarita

This is 3 parts rhubarb syrup, 2 parts tequila and 1 part Cointreau or triple sec. Shake with ice and pour into a Margarita glass – salt-rimmed, if you like.

Rhubarb 'sherbet dip-dabs'

You can serve, as an accompanying 'canapé' to any of the above cocktails, and a further affirmation of the joys of rhubarb, a few batons of freshly cut raw rhubarb arranged around a bowl of caster sugar. You dip the end of a baton into the sugar and bite off the last centimetre or so. The sour-sweet sensation is a bit like that old sweet-shop favourite, the sherbet dip-dab. In a less alcoholic context, it also makes a great treat for kids.

MAY _

Raw asparagus (and other crudités) with anchovy and caper mayonnaise__[109]_____New lettuces with 'soft-hard-boiled' eggs and spring onion__[110]_____ Lettuce risotto__[112]_____Chilled radish leaf and mint soup__[113]_____Foil-baked trout with Granary bread croûtons__[115]_____Ultimate creamed spinach__[116] Goat's cheese and yoghurt with herbs__[119]

May is the month when, in our winter reveries, we often imagine summer will be gloriously upon us. And a Sunday lunch of roast spring lamb, taken outdoors under a blinding sun, of course, will surely include a feast of just-picked baby vegetables from the garden.

But memory plays cruel tricks. May isn't quite like that. Things are coming on, without a doubt. However, like the watched pot that won't boil, our plants are snubbing our daily inspections, and progress can seem painfully slow. There's no cause for alarm. Plants have their own schedule, and simply won't be persuaded that you know any better. Unless of course you offer them a polytunnel . . . in which case you may yet have your roast spring lamb with infant peas, little-fingernail-sized broad beans and carrots no bigger than a sub-postmistress's over-sharpened pencil stub.

Polytunnels aside, May simply doesn't have the breadth of produce imagined six months previously. But what it does have can be relished without risk of hyperbole, for it is one of the year's not-to-be missed seasonal treats – asparagus. Personally, I'd hate to have fewer than half a dozen generous portions of the magic spears in the course of the season.

The trick, of course, is getting hold of the really good stuff – and that means spears that have been cut within hours rather than days. The loss of sweetness in asparagus (as with many vegetables, including peas and sweetcorn) is a simple function of time elapsed after harvest. Sugar begins to revert to starch as soon as the plant has been cut. (It can be fixed only by cooking or freezing – the latter is okay for peas and sweetcorn but pretty detrimental to the fragile texture of asparagus.) In fact, just-cut asparagus is sweet enough to eat raw, and I urge anyone who grows their own to try it like this, dipped in a simple vinaigrette, or in the anchovy and caper mayonnaise described on page 109.

That's all very well for those who grow their own, but for asparagus-lovers who have to shop for their spears the mission to find such quality specimens is more challenging. It can be done, however. Near me in Dorset is a lovely lady who grows asparagus commercially, but on a small scale. She completely understands the value of the just-cut product, and some locals will go and collect at a time when they know she'll be harvesting (deliberately or not, it often happens to coincide with the afternoon school run). Others have come to know exactly when various local stores take delivery of fresh-cut spears, and they will time their trip accordingly. Those who buy it at the local village shop will, if they time it right, be eating their asparagus within five or six hours of its being picked.

The vital sugar-to-starch time lag also explains the difference – which anyone would notice in a blind tasting – between seasonal British asparagus and the imported crop. Imported asparagus is never likely to be less than 72 hours cut by the time it reaches the supermarket, and it is probably given a use-by span of about a week, by which time it's woody, mealy and of very little interest. It staggers me that these coarse, flavourless spears continue to be flown in from Europe, America and the southern hemisphere and, expensive though they are, appear to sell in huge quantities throughout the year. The amount of food miles involved makes me want to weep.

My advice is to stick to May (and early June), and the British product. Make the effort to discover the whereabouts of your own nearest commercial asparagus grower – and bother them a lot in the month of May. Phone them and find out where they deliver to, or if you can pick up direct from them.

Incidentally, you can buy yourself a couple of extra hours' sugar by keeping your asparagus wrapped in a wet tea towel in the fridge. Our local farm shop keeps the cut stalks in a tray of water, which also seems to help. If you've managed to get hold of some good stuff but want to keep it for more than 24 hours before eating, then blanch it in boiling water for 2 minutes as soon as you get it home. Refresh it in cold water, then keep it, wrapped, in the fridge for a day or two. To serve, plunge back into boiling water for another 3–4 minutes, then serve straight away with melted butter. Or, for something a bit different, cook the

feb   mar   apr   may   jun   jul   aug   sep   oct   nov   dec

blanched spears over a barbecue, or on a very hot ridged griddle pan, for about 5 minutes, turning occasionally. Serve the char-striped spears with trickles of olive oil, a few twists of black pepper and shavings of Parmesan.

It isn't just asparagus that comes good in May. Spinach seems to forge slowly ahead whatever the weather, and by the end of the month there'll be plenty of young leaves for salads, and with a bit of luck enough more substantial ones for a first cook-up. For the first couple of outings, they'll be lightly wilted in just a little water, squeezed gently to drain off the excess, then tossed with a little butter and/or olive oil, a squeeze of lemon juice and a twist of black pepper. Then I'll make my ultimate creamed spinach (page 116).

And there's the lettuces. By the end of the month, I'd hope to be cutting one a day. One of the first to get the chop will be combined with a fresh-laid egg or two in one of my favourite early-summer salads (page 110). The arrival of the early spinach and lettuces should be reflected in good greengrocer's shops, and perhaps the supermarkets — and even if they've been grown under plastic they'll still have the edge over imported equivalents.

May's potential harvest may be more modest than hoped for but in some ways that's no bad thing. From the vegetable gardener's point of view it's still a busy month — especially for 'plug' gardeners like me (see page 64 for the hard sell). With a bit of luck, any risk of frost is past by now and, after a couple of days' hardening off, the plugs can all go out into their growing sites.

It's immensely satisfying. The pea shoots have already sprouted their first clingy tendrils, and sometimes have them wrapped around a strand of netting within hours of transplanting. The young broad beans, with their firm, waxy leaves, always seem punchy and prepared — too much of a challenge now for even the most determined slug. Even beetroot can be grown and planted this way — a hand's width apart in well-spaced grids that will not require thinning.

In the space of a single early May weekend (albeit a backbreaking one), a vast, empty expanse of chocolate-brown tilth can be transformed into a busy network of perky green seedlings. Not long now.

Raw asparagus (and other crudités) with anchovy and caper mayonnaise

If you've read the introduction to this chapter, then hopefully you've managed to get hold of some fantastically fresh English asparagus spears. The first thing to do is taste one to see if it's fresh enough to eat raw. It should be nutty, crisp, sweet and juicy. You'll either like it or you won't. If you do, then serve it alongside other raw early-summer vegetables, such as baby carrots, whole Cos lettuce leaves, immature sugar snaps and, if they're ready, raw artichokes (see page 128 for further details!).

If you think the asparagus is not quite fresh enough to eat raw, then steam or boil it for 5–12 minutes. The cooking time depends not only on its thickness but also on its freshness. Just-picked asparagus needs only a few minutes. You can serve it hot, or you can refresh it in cold water and serve cold, along with the other crudités.

The following is one of my favourite accompaniments for asparagus, raw or cooked, hot or cold. It's great with other crudités, too.

To serve 4

Combine **100ml best olive oil** with **200ml lighter oil**, such as sunflower or groundnut. Put **2 egg yolks** in a small mixing bowl (they should be at room temperature before you start). Whisk the yolks, drizzling in the mixed oils just a few drops at a time. Once the mayonnaise has taken, you can increase the flow to a steady trickle. It should be very thick and emulsified by the time you've finished adding the oil. After you have added about half the oil, loosen the mayonnaise with a squeeze of **lemon juice**.

Finely grate or mash ¼ **garlic clove** and beat it into the mayonnaise. Drain and finely chop **a small tin of anchovies**. Squeeze the excess vinegar from a generous tablespoon of **capers** (or soak, rinse and dry the salted variety), then roughly chop them. Beat the anchovies and capers into the mayonnaise, followed by a squeeze of **lemon** and a few twists of **black pepper**. Taste and adjust the lemon/pepper combination to your liking. Leave to stand for half an hour for the flavours to mingle and marry, then give it another quick whisk before serving with your selection of crudités.

feb   mar   apr   may   jun   jul   aug   sep   oct   nov   dec

New lettuces with 'soft-hard-boiled' eggs and spring onion

Those lettuces I mentioned as seedlings back in March are well on their way to maturity by now, and the picking begins in earnest. I expect to eat fresh lettuce perhaps every other day for the next few weeks, then I guess consumption slows down a bit as other vegetables come good in June.

With a bit of luck, the hens are all laying by now, and the spring grass they graze gives an extra orange intensity to their yolks. This simple dish is a seasonal celebration of these simultaneous events in the garden and on the farm — and it's one to revisit regularly throughout the summer.

To serve 4

Wash and gently dry the leaves of 2–4 lettuces (depending on size and maturity) — ideally a combination of Cos (or romaine) and butterhead types. Keep the leaves mostly whole but perhaps tear the larger ones in half.

You will need 6 eggs and they should be what I call soft-hard-boiled — i.e. the whites completely set but the yolks just a bit runny in the middle. I achieve this pretty reliably by putting them in a pan of hand-hot water, bringing it quickly to the boil and boiling the eggs for exactly 4 minutes (5 if they are extra large). Then I run them under the cold tap and peel them as soon as they are cool enough to handle.

Make a simple vinaigrette by mixing olive oil and vinegar together in a ratio of 5:1, adding a pinch of sugar, a dab of mustard and some salt and pepper and shaking it all up in a jar. Finely chop 5–6 spring onions.

Throw the lettuce leaves in a salad bowl. Roughly chop the still-warm eggs and put them with the spring onions. Pour a generous trickle of the dressing over them and mix together well. Then pile this mixture over the lettuce leaves and toss lightly. Serve at once.

Lettuce risotto

This risotto is the ultimate proof of the cookability of lettuces. The leafy butterhead types work best but you can use just about any good fresh lettuce except, I would say, iceberg. A mixture of bitter and sweet varieties (say, radicchio and Cos, or oak leaf and Clarion) will give an interesting breadth of flavours. And a smattering of tiny baby peas and spring onions sets the whole thing off nicely.

To serve 4 – 6

Pick over and roughly shred 2 large or 4 small lettuces. Slice a dozen spring onions on the diagonal into 1–2cm lengths.

Bring 1.25 litres vegetable or chicken stock to the boil, then turn the heat down to simmering point. Heat 2–3 tablespoons olive oil in a large, heavy-based pan and add 1 onion (or 2–3 shallots), finely chopped. Cook until starting to soften, then add 1 garlic clove, finely chopped, and cook for 1–2 minutes; do not allow the onion or garlic to brown. Add 350g Arborio rice to the pan, along with the spring onions, and stir well until each grain of rice is coated with oil. Pour in a ladleful of the hot stock and stir until it has been absorbed by the rice, then add another ladleful of stock. Continue to add the stock at intervals in this way, stirring all the time. After about 15 minutes, when the rice is almost done but still just a little bit chalky in the middle, add the shredded lettuce and, if you like, 100g baby peas, fresh from the polytunnel for preference (otherwise frozen). Stir gently to mix the vegetables through the rice. At first it will seem as if you have added far too much lettuce, but it will soon wilt and give up its juices to the rice. Add the last few ladlefuls of stock at this stage.

The risotto is ready when all the liquid has been absorbed, the peas are just tender and the rice is cooked (about 5 minutes after you've added the lettuce). It should be creamy, not dry. Stir in a knob of butter, then taste and adjust the seasoning. Serve immediately, offering Parmesan and a grater to your guests at the table.

Chilled radish leaf and mint soup

I adapted this recipe from one my wife cut out of a French cookery magazine. I didn't really like the recipe as described but I liked the idea, because although radishes are something I grow plenty of I hadn't ever thought of using the leaves. So I've played around with it and ended up with something I think is pretty delicious — very clean, green and refreshing — as well as thrifty. If you don't grow radishes, and can't seem to buy any with the leaves still on, then use rocket leaves instead.

To serve 4 as a light starter

Make a light vegetable stock by grating ½ onion, a carrot and a stick of celery, putting them in a pan with 250ml water and simmering gently for half an hour. Then strain and chill. Wash and trim about 20 radishes and their leaves (or use a couple of fistfuls of rocket leaves), reserving 2 nice radishes for garnish. Blanch the radishes and their leaves, along with about a dozen mint leaves, in boiling salted water for just 1 minute, then drain and refresh briefly in cold water.

Place the radishes, leaves and chilled stock in a blender with a small apple, peeled, cored and diced, 2 generous tablespoons crème fraîche, a pinch of salt, a pinch of cayenne pepper and a few twists of black pepper. Blend until smooth, green and creamy. Taste and adjust the seasoning.

Chill thoroughly in the fridge, then whisk briskly and pour into 4 small bowls or large coffee cups. Garnish with a few thin slices of raw radish and a sprinkling of chopped mint.

feb mar apr may jun jul aug sep oct nov dec

Foil-baked trout with Granary bread croûtons

May is the time to start looking out for fresh sea trout. It can be one of the great seasonal bargains on the fishmonger's slab, being every bit as good as (or better than) a fresh wild salmon and usually a fraction of the price. If your fishmonger doesn't seem to be stocking it as a matter of course, then ask him to order you one (or two, or three – I particularly like the smaller fish of under or around a kilo).

This is also a recipe to cook with any trout or sea trout you might catch. The eating quality of stocked fish, though, varies so much. In lakes, they often come out tasting muddy. As for farmed trout, most seem to me worthless: muddy and horrible. But recently I have encountered two notable exceptions. My local trout farm, in the village of Hooke (tel: 01308 862553), produces the best farmed brown trout I have ever eaten – right up there with wild chalk stream fish. I also sampled, as part of a tasting panel on Radio 4's *Food Programme*, a very palatable organic rainbow from Purely Organic (tel: 01985 841093), in Wiltshire.

Tear off 2 sheets of foil a little bit longer than your fish and lay one on top of the other. Smear the dull side of the upper sheet generously with soft butter. Prepare a few flavourings: 4–5 bay leaves, a few sprigs of thyme, a fistful of chives, a finely sliced onion. Scatter some of these over the buttered foil and lay a cleaned, gutted trout or sea trout on top. Smear a bit more butter on the fish and lay a few more of the herbs on it. Push a bay leaf, a couple of slices of onion and a knob of butter into the belly of the fish. Season well with salt and pepper. Lift up and lightly scrunch the sides and ends of the foil, so you can pour a good slosh (about 100ml) of white wine into the parcel without it leaking out.

Lay the foil parcel(s) on a baking tray and seal the foil, scrunching the 2 sides together like a Cornish pasty. Place in a hot oven (220°C/Gas Mark 7) for from 20 minutes (for a 500g fish) to 45 minutes (for a 2-kilo fish).

When the fish is nearly ready, cut a slice of malted Granary bread (ideally slightly stale) into small cubes and fry for a couple of minutes in hot oil until well browned and crisp. Drain these croûtons and keep warm.

feb   mar   apr   may   jun   jul   aug   sep   oct   nov   dec

Remove the fish from the oven and open the foil. Check it is cooked through by slipping a knife into the lateral line at the thickest part. If the flesh is still a little translucent and sticking to the bone, then re-wrap the foil and return to the oven for a few more minutes.

Carefully lift the foil parcel and strain the buttery, fishy, winey, herby juices into a small saucepan. Taste them and adjust the seasoning. This can be your sauce, unadulterated, but if you want to tart it up into something a little more formal, bring it to the boil, whisk in up to a tablespoon of double cream and boil for a minute to get a thick, glossy sauce. Finely chop a few fresh chives and stir in.

Remove the skin of the fish and lift the fillets away from the backbone. Lay these on a warmed plate, spoon over the sauce and scatter over the croûtons. Serve with plain boiled new potatoes and maybe some wilted spinach.

Ultimate creamed spinach

I adore creamed spinach. Of course, it's just chopped spinach stirred into some loose béchamel. But there are ways of bringing out the very best in a béchamel . . . When prepared like this, it's not just a side order but a dish on its own.

To serve 2 − 4

Wash and trim 500g fresh spinach, stripping out the coarse central stalks. Bring a large pan of salted water to the boil. Blanch the spinach in 3 or 4 batches, putting a good handful of leaves into the rapidly boiling water and stirring them in. Bring back to the boil and boil for just 1 minute. Remove the leaves from the water with a small sieve or slotted spoon and refresh in cold water. Then squeeze with your hands to extract as much water as you can before roughly chopping the spinach.

Grate a small onion and ½ carrot and put in a pan with 300ml whole milk, a bay leaf, a couple of twists of black pepper and a few gratings of nutmeg. Bring almost to

boiling point, then leave to infuse for 10 minutes. Strain the hot milk into a warmed jug, discarding the herbs and vegetables.

Melt **50g butter** in the pan (you don't need to wash it) and stir in **25g plain flour** to get a loose roux. Cook this gently for a couple of minutes, then add half the warm, seasoned milk and stir in. When the sauce is thick and smooth, stir in the rest of the milk. Bring to the boil and simmer gently for just a minute. Then stir in the chopped spinach. Heat through, but don't let it bubble for more than a minute. Taste and adjust the seasoning. Ladle into large, warm bowls. You can, if you like, serve with grated Parmesan, Gruyère or even Cheddar, but I think it's a purer, more spinachy dish on its own.

Goat's cheese and yoghurt with herbs

This is a dish that really smacks of spring, though it will continue to be a delight as long as you have a ready supply of fresh herbs with which to make it. You don't need a vast array, though. In fact, this is well worth making even if you have nothing more than parsley and chives on the go. The combination makes a great starter, or a snack with drinks, for that first brave, al fresco adventure of the year.

To serve 4

Use a fork to mash together **250g very fresh goat's cheese** and 3–4 tablespoons **live yoghurt** – you need to add enough yoghurt to get a loose, spoonable, but not quite pourable consistency. You only need a tiny amount of **garlic**: mash, say, a quarter of a clove with a little **salt** and mix thoroughly into the cheese. Finely chop a generous bunch of fresh herbs, majoring on masses of **parsley** and **chives** but including a little **thyme**, **marjoram**, **tarragon** and **chervil**, if they come to hand. Mix well and adjust the seasoning.

You can eat it at once, but it's best if left to ripen for an hour in a cool place. Serve with fresh crusty bread and/or a few Cos lettuce leaves and baby carrots for dipping.

feb   mar   apr   may   jun   jul   aug   sep   oct   nov   dec

JUNE_ _

June may not always be the sunfest we'd like it to be. But even when appearances suggest otherwise (i.e. when it's raining for the fifth day in a row), June has what it takes to turn May's struggling juveniles into July's productive adults. That goes for the livestock as well as the vegetables. The lambs and calves prosper on the rapidly growing pasture, and my piglets become pigs as they fatten on the roots, weeds and grass in their run, topped up with a supplement of increasingly varied garden and kitchen leftovers.

The secret of June's success is its daylight hours. Quite simply, it has more of them than any other month. Okay, only a few more than July, which will of course continue the good work. But here in Dorset it has a whole 54 minutes of daylight per day, on average, more than May. And we can all imagine what could be achieved if we added an hour to every working day.

So, however hard May works in the garden, it takes June's 4am rise and 10pm bedtime working day to finish the job. Last June, it wasn't just the sun that was up early. I found out that I was rather better at getting up early than I had previously thought. In the past, few things other than the prospect of a really exciting fishing trip could have induced me to quit the quilted cocoon before 7.15am – the rising time required to get Oscar to school.

There's only one way to discover whether you have a latent talent for early rising and that's to set your alarm for 4am and see what happens. A good motive helps. Mine was that I wanted a reasonable working day but one that was over by lunchtime, so in the afternoon I could still enjoy the long days of midsummer – in the garden, on the farm and particularly down on the coast. So that fishing trip was still a motive, but now under the very unfamiliar (to me) conditions of delayed gratification. If I was a good boy and did my work in the morning, then Marie, Oscar and I could go fishing in the afternoon.

To my great surprise, I found that not only could I handle this early start but I quickly grew to love it. My June day begins, as shards of light break the horizon, with a brisk walk around the farm, Dolly at heel, to check the livestock. They are already having their breakfast. The sheep, with glowing woolly halos backlit by the morning sun, look positively biblical. The chestnut-coloured coats of my Devon ruby cattle glisten and steam against the dewy, deep-green grass. And, as we arrive at their pen with a bucket of scraps, the pigs come cavorting to greet us with excited snuffles and puppyish leaps and headshakes. Dolly jumps into the run to join their games and is seen off by a mock charge, before bounding back only to provoke another one. Meanwhile, my Buff Orpington cockerel is regularly shrieking his arrogant, proprietorial call as his hens cluck busily and contentedly around him. Between them, my menagerie of fellow early-risers make me feel that not to be up at this time in the summer would be sheer folly.

So, after this exhilarating start to the day, and a morning of writing, I take my coastal reward and become a part-time fisherman and lobster-potter in the afternoon.

June's long days and rising temperature are felt in the sea as well as on the land. Perhaps not by the bathers on the beach. The shock of entering the water will make them catch their breath for a month or so yet. The mackerel, bream and bass, by contrast, are thoroughly excited by the subtle rise in water temperature. The lobsters and crabs are on the move, too. There is a burst of growth on the reefs and rocks of the tidal zone that will be felt all the way up the food chain. All the way to my kitchen, with a bit of luck.

The vessel for my fishing forays is a 22-foot fibreglass dory, a Wilson Flyer, with a curiously oversized wheelhouse custom-built on the deck. She's called *Sea Fox*, she's fifteen, maybe twenty, years old and was, before I bought her, both knocked about and dotingly looked after, in that contradictory style of maritime 'tough love', by a man who was secretary of the West Bay Sea Angling Club.

This distinguished provenance, quite apart from giving *Sea Fox* 'harbour cred' (something that's hard to earn down here, I can tell you), carries with it a priceless bonus: the boat's GPS system. This means that, despite having the sense of direction of a brain-damaged mole,

I can just about find my way home from a fishing trip. Even better than that, locked in its memory are over sixty 'Waypoints', giving the lat–long coordinates of many of the best fishing, potting and diving marks within a 20-mile radius of West Bay.

What a GPS doesn't do, as I soon discovered to my cost, is tell you whether after racing about the sea in breathless pursuit of shoals of June mackerel you have enough fuel left to make it back to port. Telephoning the harbour master from a mobile to confess I've run out of petrol and need to be towed in is humiliating enough. To find, on coming into port as the sun goes down, that half of West Bay has turned out on the harbour wall for an imminent midsummer firework display, is a blow to harbour cred from which I may never recover.

But at least the fishing was good. There were lobsters – not daily, but perhaps twice weekly, and frankly who could wish for more lobsters than that? We caught them in our locally made parlour pots, baited with the skeletons and guts of mackerel we had filleted. Mostly we boiled them and ate them cold with mayonnaise. A few times we boiled them only briefly to kill them, then split them down the middle and grilled them over charcoal. Then we trickled an outrageous quantity of garlic and parsley butter over the char-striped half-shells. And once I made lobster thermidor – a truly great dish (see *The River Cottage Cookbook*).

The mackerel were on tap in June and July and I don't think we had a single fishless trip. We caught them by the dozen, with plugs, spinners, feathers and spoons. Oscar loved hauling them in, his whippy little rod bent double under the strain. And he loved eating them: grilled, fried, baked, barbecued, cured, smoked and – perhaps best of all – raw, as sushi. We must have eaten hundreds over the summer and we never tired of them.

The catching, cooking and eating of these fish was a blithe family communion, the profound joy of which is hard to express. For me, part of the thrill was that Oscar seemed, unprompted, to be making that vital, respectful connection between life, death and the kitchen. It's a spark of understanding that fishing nurtures perhaps more than any other way of acquiring food.

'Daddy,' he said to me one day on the boat, 'people don't kill fish if they're not going to eat them?' This was half-statement, half-question, the syntactical ambiguity so beloved of the under-fives. 'Well,' I said hesitantly, thinking of the billions of sand eels and herrings used to make chicken feed and fertiliser, and even burned as fuel in power stations, 'they shouldn't really. But I'm afraid sometimes they do.'

Mackerel with melted onions and black olives

In Dorset, mackerel usually arrive in May or June, as they chase the sand eels and whitebait inshore, sometimes chasing them right up on to the beach. They may disappear for a few weeks in August, before returning with a vengeance to gorge on the sprats. I'll take them whenever I can get them, and never tire of eating them, whether grilled over charcoal, raw as sushi, pickled with dill, or even boiled in seawater on the beach (try it). This Provençal-style dish is one of the few 'fancy' treatments I'll allow myself – not that it's remotely difficult or time-consuming.

To serve 4 as a starter, 2 as a main course

Cut the fillets from either side of 2 whole, ungutted mackerel, as I'm doing in the photograph opposite, and season them with a little salt and pepper.

Slice 2–3 large onions – enough almost to fill a large frying pan (they will reduce to about a quarter of their volume as they cook). Heat a film of olive oil in the pan and add the onions with 3 or 4 bay leaves and a sprig or two of thyme. Sweat the onions gently, tossing and stirring frequently, for at least 10 minutes, until they are softened and golden, very tender and sweet. Don't let them burn. Add a handful of black olives, stoned and roughly chopped, and a splash of white wine. Cook for a few minutes until the wine has evaporated, then season with a little salt and pepper.

Push the onions to the edges of the pan, making space for the mackerel fillets to cook in the middle. Lay the fillets in the pan, flesh-side down. Turn them after a few minutes to cook the skin side, spreading the onions over the fish to help the transfer of heat. They should be cooked through in 7–8 minutes.

This dish can be served hot, straight from the pan, but is arguably even better at room temperature. Serve with a good chilled rosé – which will taste particularly fine with the rich, oily fish, sweet onions and salty olives.

feb   mar   apr   may   jun   jul   aug   sep   oct   nov   dec

Raw baby artichokes, and cooked adult ones

I had no idea that anyone ate artichokes raw until I visited my parents-in-law in the Loire Valley and watched in disbelief as they sat outside one sunny June lunchtime, in front of a pile of baby artichokes from the local market, and began stripping off the raw leaves. They smeared a little cold butter on the base of each leaf before nibbling. I noticed it was turning their mouths purple, but they seemed to be enjoying it so I soon joined in. It's a curious taste sensation. There's a noticeable astringency in the raw flesh, but there's also a delicious nuttiness that you don't get with cooked artichokes. I like the cold butter treatment but I also found raw artichokes very nice dipped into good olive oil with just a squeeze of lemon juice, as shown opposite.

Last summer we were spoiled with a bumper crop of our own artichokes. From June to November (we had a second flush in the mild autumn weather), we must have had over 50 off just seven plants. We had our fair share of little ones, which we ate raw, and plenty of hefty ones too, which we boiled or steamed. I found that, like asparagus and purple sprouting broccoli, the shorter the interval between picking and cooking, the shorter the cooking time necessary. Even the biggest ones didn't need more than 6 minutes' boiling, if plunged into the pan within an hour of picking.

Our favourite treatment for the hot ones was to dip the leaves in a bowl of melted salted butter seasoned with a little black pepper and spiked with a few drops of lemon juice and a little cayenne pepper.

One evening I felt we were rich enough in artichokes to make up a salad I remembered from my days sous-cheffing at the River Café in London. The thickly sliced hearts of half a dozen artichokes (from which we'd already eaten all the leaves) were tossed with warm new potatoes, a knob of butter, the very best olive oil and a few shavings of Parmesan. At the River Café, a squirt of truffle oil would also be added, but the dish is a delight even without this extravagance.

Baby broad beans with chorizo

If I had to name my favourite first harvest of the year, I think it would be the baby broad beans. Try as I might, I can't resist attacking the pods when the beans inside are scarcely bigger than my little fingernail. After a few portions of lightly cooked infants adorned only with a little melted butter, I'll move on to some simple combinations – and thin slivers of lightly fried chorizo is one of my favourites.

To serve 2 as a starter

Cook about **250g baby broad beans** in boiling salted water for just 2 minutes, then drain. Finely slice **a 100g piece of spicy Spanish chorizo**. Heat 1 tablespoon olive oil in a small pan and fry the chorizo in it for a minute or so, until lightly crisp. Throw the broad beans in the pan and toss with the chorizo for a minute, so the beans are heated through and coated with the spicy oil. Serve at once.

- -

Crushed strawberries and cream

This is just a little twist on the great summer classic, which I happen to think makes it even more delectable. For a further twist, where the freezer comes into play, see over the page.

To serve 4

Take at least **500g best English strawberries** and, as you hull them, set aside the best (i.e. least blemished) half. Crush the other half in a bowl with a fork, rub through a nylon sieve and sweeten to taste by whisking in up to **50g icing sugar**. Stir in a modest splash of **balsamic or other aged vinegar**. Slice the reserved strawberries into 3 or 4 pieces each and mix with the sweetened purée. Chill thoroughly. Divide between 4 bowls and swirl a good tablespoon of **double cream** over each.

feb   mar   apr   may   jun   jul   aug   sep   oct   nov   dec

Strawberry granita

If you don't have an ice-cream machine, an easy way to make delicious fresh fruit ices is to freeze your sweetened fruit pulp solid in a tray and scratch it up into frosty shards with a strong fork just before serving. This is what Italians would call a granita. The texture is a little crunchier than a classic sorbet, but still wonderful. In fact, even though I have an excellent machine, I often make this strawberry granita in preference to a smoother sorbet. It's sweet, tart, fruity and endlessly refreshing.

To serve 6 – 8

Crush a kilo of strawberries and rub them through a nylon sieve to extract the seeds. Whisk in up to 200g icing sugar and the juice of 1–2 lemons to sweeten and sharpen to taste. The mix should be a little too sweet and a little too sharp, to allow for the fact that both tastes will be muted slightly when it is frozen.

Pour the purée into a bowl or large Tupperware tub, ideally so it is no deeper than about 4cm, so it will freeze quickly. Put in the freezer until solid. Defrost for about half an hour before serving, then use a robust fork to scrape up the surface of the frozen fruit, piling the frosty shards into glasses. Serve quickly, before it has time to melt.

Variation: Snow-capped granita

My editor, Richard Atkinson, told me that he always serves his granitas with a couple of tablespoonfuls of double cream poured over the top. The granita must be cold enough to freeze the cream into a solid 'snow cap'.

I have tried it and confirm that it is an excellent suggestion – especially if the cream is ever so slightly sweetened with a little icing sugar.

Gooseberry ice-cream

The first hard, sharp gooseberries are likely to be the first fruit harvest of the year, beating even the strawberries, and by the end of June they'll be coming thick and fast. They're such an under-exploited fruit — perhaps because they are so unappealing in their raw state. But once heat and a little sugar have released their full tart but aromatic flavour they are transformed. I adore them, and they make one of the best ice-creams I know.

To serve 6 — 8

Place 1 kilo of gooseberries in a saucepan with a dribble of water to get them started and 125g caster sugar. Stir over a low heat until the sugar has dissolved. Bring to a gentle simmer and cook for about 10–15 minutes, until the gooseberries are completely soft and mostly broken. Rub the mixture through a sieve into a bowl.

Measure 500ml double cream and combine half of it with 250ml whole milk. Scald this mixture in a pan until almost boiling. Mix 4 egg yolks with 125g caster sugar, then pour in the hot milk and cream, whisking all the time. Return this custard to the pan and stir constantly over a very gentle heat until it starts to thicken. Remove from the heat and keep stirring as it cools and thickens further.

Combine the custard with the sieved gooseberry purée, mixing thoroughly. Lightly whip the remaining double cream and fold it in. You've pretty much made a rich gooseberry fool, and you could chill it and serve it as such at this point — or press on and make your ice-cream. Taste the mixture and add more sugar if you think it needs it. An ice-cream mixture before freezing should always taste a little too sweet, as sweetness is muted in the freezing process.

Now either pour the mixture into an ice-cream machine and churn until frozen or freeze-churn the old-fashioned way, by putting the mixing basin in the freezer and removing it every hour or so to whisk up and emulsify the half-frozen mixture.

Pack into tubs and freeze. Leave at room temperature for a good half an hour before serving. Serve with shortbread or other sweet biscuits, or as an accompaniment to the next recipe, whose heat will cause it to melt tantalisingly on the plate . . .

Elderflower fritters

If you've never made elderflower fritters, I beg you to. They're an absolute delight.

To serve 4

First make the batter. Mix 125g plain flour with a pinch of salt, 25g caster sugar, 2 tablespoons olive oil and 1 tablespoon rum or kirsch. Whisk in up to 150ml water, stopping when the batter has the consistency of very thick paint; it needs to be thick enough to hold a couple of stiffly whisked egg whites. Cover and leave to stand in a cool place for at least 30 minutes.

Choose 8 large, fresh and fragrant sprays of elderflower and give them a quick bug check, but handle them as little as possible, as you want the fragrant pollen to stay in the flowers. (It may be excessive caution, but I try to carry them flowerhead-up.)

In a large, high-sided pan (or a deep-fat fryer) heat at least 5cm of good frying oil, such as groundnut or sunflower, until a small cube of white bread thrown into it turns golden brown in about a minute. Turn down the heat to maintain a steady temperature.

Whisk 2 egg whites until they form soft peaks, then gently fold them into the batter. Dip the flowers in the batter, allowing the excess to drip off them, then lower them gently into the hot oil. Fry in batches of 2 or 3, turning once or twice, until they are puffed up and golden brown. Remove each as soon as it is done and drain on kitchen paper. Keep in a low oven or on a warm plate until you have enough to serve.

Pile on a plate and sprinkle with a little caster sugar. Serve with lemon wedges to squeeze over them. Or, for a seriously indulgent seasonal treat, serve with a scoop of gooseberry ice-cream (see opposite), nuzzling up and melting into the 2 fritters.

- -

feb   mar   apr   may   jun   jul   aug   sep   oct   nov   dec

JULY_ _

July is the opposite of February – and that can only be a good thing. No need for ingenuity and effort. No seasonal despondency to cook your way out of. This is the moment you've been waiting for: a glorious harvest of sun-ripened vegetables and fruits to be enjoyed in all their unadorned nakedness.

If you're not lucky enough to have your own vegetable garden, then this is the month to do business with those who have. This is as good as fresh fruit and vegetables get, and you'd be a fool not to claim your fair share: so get to the local farmers' market, a farm shop or a pick-your-own premises without delay.

Incidentally, I often wonder why so few PYO fruit farms have extended this admirable method of retailing fresh produce to include vegetables. There are surely enough people who appreciate the difference in taste, and the sheer feel-good factor, of just-picked vegetables to make this a very viable commercial proposition. People who dream of having their own vegetable patch but just can't find the time to make it happen. You'd go, wouldn't you?

I know what pleasures could be had from such an enterprise because from July until September this is exactly what is happening in my garden. We practically live among the vegetables. Any July day on which more hours are spent inside than out is, in my book, a day misspent. 'Supper' may simply mean cruising through the garden for an hour or so, eating raw peas, broad beans, carrots and lettuces until we can't manage any more.

Forays into the kitchen are purely for a rapid combination of absurdly fresh ingredients, and perhaps for shaking up a hastily improvised dressing. If heat is applied at all, it is the briefest of blanchings, to fix the natural sugars of something picked just minutes before. And when the 'cooking' is done, with a bit of luck the dish comes out of the kitchen and heads back into the garden, where it belongs. Al fresco at every opportunity is our July motto.

If only, one is left thinking, it were possible to bottle July's bounty for leisurely consumption at less plentiful times of year. It is, of course. And these days the most practical way metaphorically to 'bottle' the harvest is to freeze it.

This raises the question of whether it goes against the spirit of seasonal cooking to freeze the excess of the harvest so it can be used when it is no longer in season. To my mind, there's only one answer: it would be mad not to. It's not out of some puritanical sense of self-denial that I've been urging you to think seasonally in this book. It's because, almost by definition, seasonal local food is likely to be fresher and tastier than unseasonal imported food. So the philosophical freezing question is simply this: can the produce in question, once frozen, still compete – either with its fresh self or with what is available fresh at the time of year you might wish to defrost it?

There are many vegetables for which the answer is a resounding no. Carrots, French and runner beans, beetroot, broccoli, cabbages, cauliflower – all of these return from the freezer to the table like zombies from the grave. Which is to say they don't look half as good as they did when they were alive, and encounters with them in the flesh, or what's left of it, are simply not pleasant. This is usually due to loss of texture. Of course when vegetables are transformed into soups and purées (including, very usefully we have found, baby food), texture is no longer an issue and freezing becomes a sound option.

However, there are two vegetables in particular that survive the process of being frozen whole and intact remarkably well. In fact, their defrosted self is so winning that even those familiar with the original would struggle to spot that they'd been frozen at all.

I'm talking about peas and broad beans. Worth freezing not only because they freeze well but also because, in my book, they are two of the most delicious vegetables on the planet. So the 'can they compete?' question is also a no-brainer. Peas from the freezer? In January? With steak and kidney pudding? Yes please!

I see no sacrilege here. For many a year now, my father has had a ritual of reserving the last batch of frozen broad beans to serve, alongside the sprouts and parsnips, with the goose on Christmas Day. Long may it continue – he won't hear a murmur of complaint from me.

feb   mar   apr   may   jun   jul   aug   sep   oct   nov   dec

The success of the reincarnated pea and broad bean does, however, depend on the freezing technique. The most important thing to remember is that the aim is principally to fix the sugars. The best way to do this is to pick, pod, blanch and drop in the freezer all within an hour – two at the most. Blanching simply means immersing the peas or beans in rapidly boiling water for about a minute. Then drain them, refresh quickly in ice-cold water, toss in a tea towel to dry, and bag up for the freezer. Sucking the air out of the bag – either with your own lungs or, if you're freezing a big harvest, with a vac-packing machine – helps to remove moist air that will otherwise form ice crystals that can damage the peas or beans.

When it comes to reincarnation, bring a pan of lightly salted water to a rolling boil. Peel off the bag from the still-frozen peas and add them to the pan. Once the water has come back to the boil, a scant minute is all the peas or beans will need – from which you may correctly deduce that I would never cook fresh young garden peas or broad beans for longer than two minutes. You could make that four or five for fatter, older peas and beans – but no more.

Get this right and you will have something that is beaten only by the taste of the very same, just-picked peas a few minutes before they went in the freezer. It's as well not to fool oneself about this. It is, I'm afraid, out of a quite misguided sense of virtue – to thank them, I guess, for at least trying – that I sometimes find myself gathering up from a greengrocer's box the withered shells of some peas-in-the-pod that have been languishing there for days. I know in my heart of hearts that, when it comes to taste, Birds Eye will have them licked every time.

Turning our attention from vegetables to fruit for a moment, which is something we certainly shouldn't forget to do this month, we may apply the freezing question again. Which of July's abundant soft fruits and berries are worth freezing? The answer is that if you wish to reincarnate the fruit, like the pea or the broad bean, as some passable vestige of its former self, then only one type of summer fruit passes the test: the raspberry, and its related cluster-berry types, the tayberry and loganberry. Freeze these as individuals on trays. Then, when they are frozen as solid as stones, pack them loose in Tupperware boxes. Spread them out in an even, single layer to defrost and they'll be passably usable as fresh fruit.

It is worth amending the question, though, to broaden the catchment: which summer fruits are worth freezing as purées or, better still, sorbets and ice-creams? The answer is, all that you can possibly lay your hands on.

French beans with tapenade and chicken

I'm very keen on French beans, but on balance I prefer them cold to hot, especially on a sunny day. This dish is a lovely, crunchy summer salad, a kind of variation on the Niçoise theme, that you could easily take on a picnic. It's very easy to put together – and it's one of my favourite dishes in the whole book.

To serve 2 as a light meal, 4 as a starter

To make the tapenade, chop **125g stoned black olives** (the Kalamata type works well) with **1 garlic clove**, **½–1 small red chilli**, depending on heat, and **a dozen anchovy fillets**. Keep chopping, with a large blade or a mezzaluna, until everything is very finely chopped but not quite a purée. Mix with 2 tablespoons **good olive oil**.

Top and tail about **500g young, fresh French beans** (several different varieties, if you like), then steam or boil them for 4–5 minutes, so they are just tender but still *al dente*. Refresh in cold water, then drain and shake in a tea towel to dry. Chop or tear up to **500g leftover roast chicken** into bite-sized strips.

Put the chicken, beans and tapenade into a bowl and toss thoroughly together.

- -

Beetroot, rocket and feta salad

The gardening guru and vegetable expert, Sarah Raven, first served me this salad and I've made it dozens of times since. It's a classic combination of contrasting textures and flavours: sweet and crunchy from the beetroot; hot and leafy from the rocket; salty and crumbly from the feta. And it can all be put together in a matter of minutes.

The beetroot–feta combination is worth experimenting with – I have found it works beautifully in a chilled beetroot soup (see *The River Cottage Cookbook*). And note also that salty blue cheeses, such as Roquefort and our local Dorset Blue Vinney, make an interesting alternative to the feta in both cases.

feb   mar   apr   may   jun   jul   aug   sep   oct   nov   dec

To serve 4 as a starter

Wash and peel **500g beetroot** – preferably baby ones that you can keep whole, otherwise cut them into 3cm chunks. Simmer gently, or steam, for 7–10 minutes, until tender but still a little crunchy. Leave to cool.

Put **a couple of handfuls of rocket leaves** in a salad bowl with the beetroot, then crumble **125g feta cheese** on top. Dress with 2 tablespoons **best olive oil**, a good squeeze of **lemon juice** and a few twists of **black pepper**. Toss well together and serve.

- -

Baby peas with ham and garlic

This simple dish takes seconds to make and produces one of the most scintillating flavour combinations I know. It also works well with baby broad beans, or a mixture of beans and peas.

Take a few thin slices of **dry-cured ham**, such as Parma or Serrano, and cut them roughly into little pieces (or use a few rashers of dry-cured streaky bacon or pancetta). Blanch some **baby peas** in lightly salted boiling water for just 1 minute, then drain. Heat some **oil** in a small pan and add some fine slices of **garlic** – a couple of cloves' worth. As soon as this starts to take colour (within a minute, probably), add the ham. Continue frying for another couple of minutes until the ham is not-quite-crispy, then add the peas. Sauté together for a minute or so, shaking the pan occasionally to mix well.

Shake on to plates and eat straight away. You can toss the combination with pasta, such as penne, to make a supper of it.

- -

Sugar snaps with sesame seeds

The sugar snap pea is, I feel, a great improvement on the rather miserly mangetout. You get the best of both worlds – a pod you can eat, with a litter of beautiful baby peas suckling inside it. This is just about the easiest recipe in the book. The sesame seed treatment is only one of several variations on the theme – lightly toasted and crushed cashew nuts, or peanuts, or other seeds such as sunflower or pumpkin, can all be used.

To serve 2 as a starter, 4 as a side dish

Strip off the tough vein on the inside curve of about 500g sugar snap peas. Boil or steam them for just 3–4 minutes, then drain. Toast 1 tablespoon sesame seeds in a dry pan over a medium heat, till they colour lightly and smell nutty. Throw the sugar snaps into the pan, add 1 tablespoon toasted sesame oil and a few shakes of soy sauce, then shake the pan to coat the pods thoroughly.

Serve at once, as a course on its own or as a side dish, particularly alongside fish.

- -

Baby courgette salad

Courgettes must be young and firm if they are to be eaten raw – ideally just picked. This very simple salad shows them to their best advantage.

To serve 2 as a starter

Wash and dry about 200g baby courgettes and cut them into ½–1cm rounds. Finely chop a few mint leaves, and a couple of sprigs of marjoram or oregano if handy. Put everything in a salad bowl and add 3 tablespoons olive oil, 1 tablespoon lemon juice, a few twists of black pepper and a sprinkling of flaky salt. Toss well together. Sprinkle a handful of lightly toasted pine nuts on top and serve.

feb   mar   apr   may   jun   jul   aug   sep   oct   nov   dec

Blackcurrant double-ripple ice-cream

Blackcurrants are so intensely flavoured that you don't need much of their purée to make an ice-cream. This recipe keeps the purée very tart and sharp. Half of it is used to flavour a classic, custard-based ice-cream, while the other half makes ripples of very intense, concentrated fruit purée. It's a tantalising, sherbety, sweet-and-sour effect.

To serve 6 – 8

Place **600g blackcurrants** in a saucepan with a dribble of water to get them started and **50g caster sugar**. Stir over a low heat until the sugar has dissolved. Bring to a gentle simmer and cook for 10–15 minutes, until the blackcurrants are completely soft and the juices have run. Rub the mixture through a sieve into a bowl and chill.

Measure **500ml double cream** and combine half of it with **250ml whole milk**. Scald this mixture in a pan until almost boiling. Mix **4 egg yolks** with **125g caster sugar**, then pour the hot milk and cream on to them, whisking all the time. Return this custard to the pan and stir constantly over a very gentle heat until it starts to thicken. Take off the heat and keep stirring as it cools and thickens further.

Combine the custard with half the blackcurrant purée, mixing thoroughly. Lightly whip the remaining 250ml double cream and fold it in. Taste the mixture and add more sugar if you think it needs it. An ice-cream mixture before freezing should always taste a little too sweet, as sweetness is muted in the freezing process.

Now either pour the mixture into an ice-cream machine and churn until nearly frozen or freeze-churn the old-fashioned way by putting the mixing bowl in the freezer and removing every hour or so to whisk up and emulsify the half-frozen mixture. Whichever route you choose, when the ice-cream is thick enough to hold its shape but soft enough to work a little, spread it in a large mixing basin and make several channels, grooves and holes in it. Into these, trickle little pools of the remaining blackcurrant purée. Cut and turn the mixture a few times to spread these ripples around, but don't overdo it, or they'll get too mixed up with the ice-cream. The aim is to create a contrast of both colour and taste.

Pack into tubs and freeze. Leave at room temperature for a good half-hour before serving. Serve with shortbread or other sweet biscuits, including the lavender shortbread on page 151.

Verbena lemonade

Although its vital ingredient is almost impossible to buy in the shops, I include this recipe because I reckon it is a contender for the most refreshing summer drink of all time. That ingredient is the culinary herb lemon verbena, *Aloysia triphylla*, not to be confused with the popular hanging basket/bedding flower also called verbena. So if you want to experience this delight you'll have to grow the herb yourself. But it's easy to cultivate, and does well in a pot, too, so even urbanites and high-rise dwellers could grow it in a windowbox or in a container on a fire escape or patio.

It can be a little difficult to get started from seed, so my advice is to buy a small pot (or two) of the growing plant from a good garden centre and grow it on. Buy it in the spring and you'll get a small crop the first summer, and plenty the following year. It's a vigorous, shrubby herb that likes a sunny but sheltered spot, and should be protected from harsh frosts (keep it in a pot and you can bring it indoors).

To make 1 litre

Crush a few sprigs of **lemon verbena leaves** in your hand and put them into a warmed teapot or jug. Add 2 tablespoons **sugar** and pour over 1 litre of boiling water. Stir to dissolve the sugar, then leave to cool. Strain this sweetened, scented infusion and store it in a sealed bottle in the fridge for up to a week, until you want to use it.

To serve the lemonade, squeeze some **fresh lemons** and mix with the cold infusion to taste, then pour over ice in a tall glass. Add a couple of bruised fresh leaves, if you like.

Variation: Lemon verbena sorbet/granita

Make a syrup by putting **125g caster sugar** in a pan with 500ml water, heating gently to dissolve, then boiling hard for 3 minutes. Remove from the heat and add a couple of fistfuls of well-bruised **lemon verbena** and the juice and zest of **2–3 lemons**. Strain when cool, then freeze and churn (for a sorbet) or freeze solid then scratch into shards with a fork (for a granita).

Lavender shortbread

Lavender is quite a trendy flavouring at the moment, which doesn't instantly endear it to me, and I had a lavender *crème brûlée* recently that I felt didn't work at all. However, I do love these simple, summer-scented biscuits. And as lavender is so popular and prolific in English gardens it seems a pity not to put it to good work in the kitchen.

Most lavender varieties flower from early July and all are suitable for culinary use. Sprigs can also be hung up and dried in a warm kitchen or airing cupboard, then kept in sealed boxes or bags for winter use, too. Their potency will slowly fade over time, but not before a fresh crop is flowering the following year.

This shortbread is good on its own but particularly fine as an accompaniment to tart fruit ices, such as strawberry granita (page 132) or gooseberry ice-cream (page 134).

To make 12–20 fingers

Beat together **160g softened unsalted butter, 80g caster sugar** and 2 teaspoons **fresh lavender flowers** (or 1 teaspoon dried lavender) until pale and creamy. Sift in **240g plain flour** – or **160g plain flour and 80g cornflour**, as some shortbread aficionados prefer – and work to a smooth dough. Alternatively you could just mix everything together in a food processor or with an electric mixer. Turn the mixture into a greased rectangular tin, about 18 x 28cm, and press it out into an even layer. Prick all over with a fork, pushing the fork right through the dough. Bake at 170°C/Gas Mark 3 for 20–25 minutes, until very lightly coloured and just firm to the touch. Remove from the oven, sprinkle with **caster sugar** and mark into fingers by pressing a couple of millimetres into the still-soft biscuit with the blade of a knife. Leave to cool and harden, then carefully break through the knife marks into fingers.

feb   mar   apr   may   jun   jul   aug   sep   oct   nov   dec

AUGUST_____

We are spoiled by nature, and spoiled by Nature. July's abundance is thrilling, but within a few weeks we may be swamped by the sheer fecundity of the harvest. We have perhaps already forgotten the tremulous excitement with which individual seeds rolled off our fingertips into a plug of lightly tamped compost back in the polytunnel in March. And the child-like thrill with which we cracked the first pea pod has given way to the glutton's nonchalance. Instead of savouring such little miracles, we have begun stomping about the garden, cursing the thigh-sized marrows that were meant to be courgettes and the rusty broad bean pods now fat enough to serve as sleeping bags for plump field mice.

'What the hell am I supposed to do with all this stuff?' we ask. But we shouldn't whinge. This is the kind of problem that half the world dreams of. So we must avoid these negative vibrations and get on top of our crop without delay. Make the harvest daily, of at least three different kinds of vegetable, and ring the changes. Pick double quantities – one for dinner and one for the freezer.

Don't despair at the cannonball peas in their whitening, wrinkled pods – suckling babes turned OAPs in a matter of weeks. Don't scorn the overgrown lettuces either, even if they have almost gone to seed. Put these two together and even in old age they are, with the support of a trusty old onion, still capable of romance. Pea and lettuce soup is as much a pleasure to defrost and heat up for a warming winter supper as it is to chill down and sip at on a stifling August evening. And more crudely, a coarse pea purée, with a bit of ham or bacon, makes one of my all-time favourite summer suppers (page 164).

There will be casualties. I thought my romanesco cauliflower was meant to be an autumn staple, but much of it had bolted by mid-August. It is certainly a little easier to forgive yourself for squandering such richness if you keep pigs. The first of our three went to slaughter in mid-August for a spit-roast – the centrepiece of a memorable camping weekend for our friends and Oscar's. Before she died, she feasted on the pods of our almost-daily crop of peas and broad beans. I think it was the finest roast pork I have ever tasted, and I credit the high-summer vegetable garden diet as much as the wood fire and the spit.

There's certainly a lot to get your head around this month. Last year potatoes and tomatoes seemed to occupy more than their fair share of my gardening brain. The gardener has a love–hate relationship with these two, and August is often the month where both emotions are most intensely felt. Throughout July they seem like the most vigorous and indestructible of plants. But a few musty days in August can release the spores of blight that weaken them fatally.

Here in Dorset, potato blight seems to be not an occasional disease but an annual inevitability, earlier and worse in some years than others. Blight management is the name of the game. I'll share my understanding of it because I only really got the hang of it last year.

When the first browning starts to appear on the leaves of one plant, you can kid yourself it's just a little scarring or scorching. When it begins to spread to the surrounding plants at a steady and even rate, you know what's happening. But there's no need to panic. There is a merciful lag between the infection of leaves by airborne spores and the blighting and rotting of the tubers below. Even as the green leaves wither and die, the potatoes will continue to thrive and grow. But you really don't want to miss the crossing point. As soon as the majority of plants in a given row are showing more withered and brown leaves than fresh and green ones, you should cut down the whole row, just an inch or two above the ground. Drastic, I know, but the idea is to kill off the blight before it infects and rots the tubers. Remove all the cut foliage from the area. You can compost it, but it should be buried under a thick layer of existing compost or grass cuttings, to suffocate and kill the spores.

You should then leave the potatoes in the ground, harvesting as you need them, for at least ten days but no more than 20 (fewer if the ground is wet). In this time frame any residual blight spores should die off before the tubers are infected and begin to rot. Whatever

feb   mar   apr   may   jun   jul   aug   sep   oct   nov   dec

is left must then be lifted and stored. Lift on a dry day if you can, and leave the tubers for a few hours on the surface. If the weather thwarts you, transfer them to a warm kitchen on newspaper. The point is that they are best stored 'dirty but dry' – in wooden or cardboard boxes, covered, in a cool place.

Tomato blight is less inevitable. Look after your plants well and you may not be troubled by it. But when it comes, it is faster and more devastating than when it hits the potatoes.

I'm afraid I messed up again last summer, for the second time in four years. Delighted with my new polytunnel, I was keen to try a whole bunch of new varieties. I grew a ridiculous number of plants in pots from seed, and although I gave a lot away I still tried to cram in too many and I planted them out, I now realise, far too close together. Had I been more ruthless with my pinching out and stripping, I might have got away with it. Instead I revelled in the rude health and magnificent foliage of my tomato plants throughout May, June and July, and was delighted to see so many flowers, which quickly turned into trusses of embryonic fruit.

July was humid and often windless. My dad, a very successful tomato grower, came to see us one weekend and was appalled by the scenes of lushness in the polytunnel – pride waiting for a fall. We did a radical panic prune, reducing the foliage by about half. But even such harsh measures proved too little too late. By the first week in August, blight was appearing on the leaves before a single fruit was ripe. And a couple of weeks later, much of the green fruit was already scarred with the brown bruises of blight.

An exercise in cutting your losses is all that is left to try. You can delay the inevitable, and give a few more tomatoes the chance to ripen before they succumb, by stripping off all the foliage (yes, every single leaf and stem that isn't a fruit-bearing vine). You can also do a massive pick of your biggest, unblighted green tomatoes and derive some comfort from a huge batch of chutney. We did both these things, and managed to salvage enough of a crop for our immediate gratification. In the end we ate most of our tomatoes as fresh fruit, in August. By the middle of September it was all over, and we'd probably only been able to harvest a third of our potential crop. There's no luscious tomato purée in the freezer this winter.

Lesson learned. Next year I'm going to be super-cautious Mr Conscientious tomato grower. Am I capable of such discipline? Marie points out that I've already acquired about 20 different varieties of tomato seeds for the coming year. Get a grip, Hugh, get a grip . . .

Courgette and goat's cheese soup with basil

When the courgettes start to get really prolific and you've already had them raw, fried, grilled and every which way, this is a great dish to help you get on top of the glut. Warm or chilled, it makes a lovely starter, and is well worth buying for if you don't share the glut problem of those of us who grow.

To serve 4 – 5

Slice a good kilo of firm courgettes into rounds, about coin-thickness. Heat 2–3 tablespoons olive oil in a large saucepan and add 2 finely chopped cloves of garlic. Just as the garlic starts to colour, add the courgettes. Cook them gently, on what I like to call a 'slow sizzle', so that they soften without browning. Continue cooking, stirring or tossing frequently, until the courgettes are completely soft and almost all their water has evaporated; this may take 20 minutes or more. Then bash to a pulpy consistency (a rough purée) with a potato masher – or pulse a few times in a food processor if you prefer.

Beat in 3–4 tablespoons fresh goat's cheese, until well mixed with the courgettes. Pour in up to 750ml hot milk, a little at a time, stirring well, until the soup reaches the desired consistency (I like it fairly thick). Bring the soup scarcely to boiling point, season to taste with salt and pepper and serve at once, with a trickle of good olive oil and a few torn basil leaves strewn over each bowl.

You can also serve the soup chilled. To chill it rapidly, transfer to a basin and put the basin in a larger bowl of ice cubes and cold water. Stir the soup until thoroughly chilled, changing the water and ice if necessary. Serve with olive oil and basil, as above.

feb   mar   apr   may   jun   jul   aug   sep   oct   nov   dec

Half-the-garden soup

For me, this is sheer delight – a celebration of all those fantastic things coming ready in the garden at the same time. The great thing about it is that no stock is necessary, as the vegetables give plenty of flavour to the liquor, and no single ingredient is truly essential – although I might feel a little compromised without the tomatoes and onions. Basically, as long as you can put together at least half a dozen of the ingredients suggested below, you'll make a sensational soup. Variations of this soup go right through to late October.

To serve 4 – 6

Slice a good **500g onions** and sweat them in a little **olive oil or butter** in a large pan until softened. Pour boiling water over ½–1 **kilo ripe tomatoes**, leave for a minute, then drain and peel off the skins. Chop roughly and add to the onions. Cook gently until thick and pulpy, then add about 500ml cold water (or light stock) and a good pinch of **salt**. Now add some or all of the following: 3–4 **medium carrots**, diced, 3–4 **medium beetroot**, diced, 3–4 **medium courgettes**, diced, a few handfuls of **peas** and a fistful of **French or runner beans**, roughly chopped. Bring to the boil and simmer for 10 minutes. Then add either or (preferably) both of the following: a fistful of **chard or spinach leaves**, finely shredded, and a fistful of **kale or cabbage leaves**, finely shredded. Top up with a little more boiling water if you like. Simmer for another 5 minutes, stirring regularly, until all the vegetables are tender, but only just. Check and adjust the seasoning, then serve immediately, with a trickle of **olive oil** over each bowl.

Seasonal variations

From late August onwards you can add fresh podded **haricot beans** (i.e. the white beans inside overgrown French beans) **or borlotti beans**, or the beans from overgrown runners, to the soup. They should go in with the water and have a good 5-minute simmer before the carrots *et al* go in. Or you can cheat by simply adding tinned beans or chickpeas.

By late October **pumpkins** and **squashes** come into play, as do **leeks, salsify** and **parsnips**. You can also bulk this soup out by adding torn-up chunks of **stale bread** (ciabatta or similar), tossed in olive oil, at the same time as the shredded greens.

Beetroot consommé

Only two ingredients here, bar the salt and pepper, yet this is an elegant dish that I wouldn't hesitate to serve at even the most formal dinner. For such an occasion I'd use a properly clarified stock, but a more homely version can also be knocked up with a less fancy stock — with a bit of pasta and maybe even leftover chicken or beef thrown in to make a meal of it.

The beetroot will add sweetness and body to the stock, but the stock should be well flavoured to start with. If necessary, boil to reduce it until the flavour is right.

To serve 4 as a light starter

Peel and rinse **500g small beetroot** and cut them into thin matchsticks (I use the smallest setting on my plastic mandoline). Bring **1 litre good, strong beef or chicken stock** to a gentle simmer, add the beetroot matchsticks and bring back to the boil. Don't let it cook any further, but adjust the seasoning and serve at once, in warmed bowls.

- -

Barbecued August vegetables

Marinated grilled vegetables have been 'trendy' for so long now that they're about as cool as your dad at the wedding disco. That doesn't mean they've become any less delicious. But forget about peppers and aubergines (unless you've been a clever clogs and grown them yourself in a greenhouse or polytunnel). Get to grips with what is seasonal in the English vegetable garden in high summer: spring onions and/or tender young leeks, various French beans, courgettes, the first fennel bulbs, even thin slices of beetroot.

To serve 4

Light the barbecue (or heat a ridged griddle pan over a medium heat). Top and tail **a fistful of French beans** and trim **8–12 spring onions or baby leeks**. Blanch the beans and spring onions or leeks in boiling salted water for just 2 minutes, then drain, refresh in cold

feb   mar   apr   may   jun   jul   aug   sep   oct   nov   dec

water and pat dry. Trim the ends off **250g courgettes** and slice lengthways into batons – these may be half sections if the courgettes are fairly tiny, quarters if they are medium, or sixths or eighths if they are on the large side. Peel and thinly slice **3–4 young beetroot** to about 10p-piece thickness, and slice **1–2 fennel bulbs** to a similar thickness.

When the barbecue is ready (i.e. red-hot glowing coals with no flames), or the griddle pan is very hot, spread the vegetables in batches over the grill, turning after a minute or so when they are lightly char-striped on one side. Then remove when the other side is done, transferring them to a large plate or shallow salad bowl. Put on the next batch and, while it is cooking, dress the still-warm batch with a trickle of **olive oil** and a squeeze of **lemon juice**, plus a pinch of **coarse salt** and a twist of **black pepper**. As you add subsequent batches of grilled vegetables to the first, add a little more oil and lemon juice and adjust the seasoning. Toss all the grilled vegetables together one last time and leave for a few minutes before serving.

You can either serve them, classically, on bruschetta (grilled bread rubbed with garlic and trickled with olive oil). Or, which is my preference, accompany with warm new potatoes.

- -

Bacon or ham with fresh pea purée

This is my dish for using up those fat cannonball peas that inevitably escape the attention of even the wiliest picker. They are a bit mealy and starchy compared to their baby cousins but, simmered in the salty-sweet ham stock until completely tender, they whizz up to a delicious purée of satisfying depth and freshness.

My favourite piece of meat for this recipe is a good chunk of salt belly or pancetta with the skin still on. But any piece of boiling ham or gammon will work well.

In the winter you can make exactly the same dish using split green or yellow peas, though they'll take much longer to cook and you'll need to keep adding the ham stock, risotto style, to stop them boiling dry.

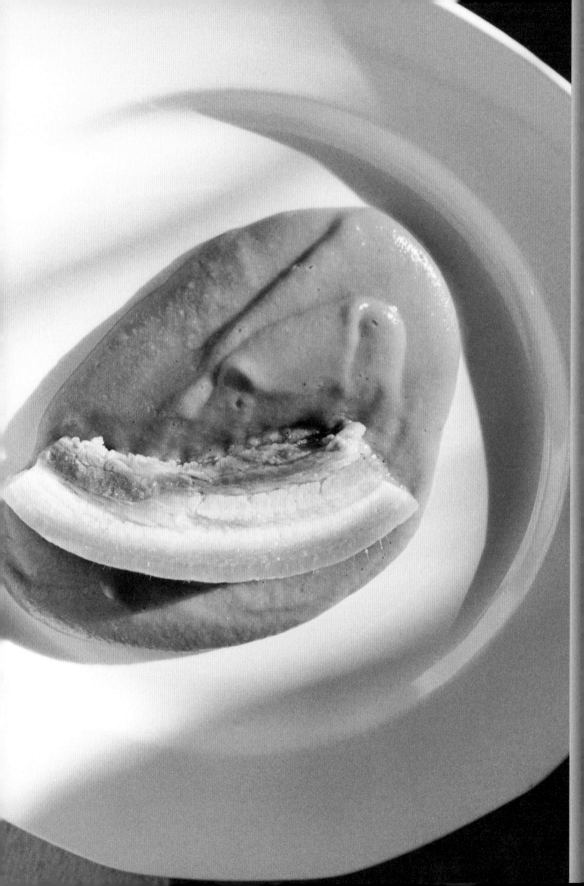

To serve 5 – 6

Take a piece of bacon or ham weighing about 1 kilo (pre-soaked in fresh water for a few hours if very salty) and place in a saucepan with a few roughly chopped stock vegetables, such as carrots, onions and celery, and a bay leaf. Bring to the boil and simmer gently for up to 2 hours, until the meat is completely tender. Put 750g fresh or frozen peas in a small pan and ladle over just enough stock from cooking the ham to cover them. You can, if you like, add a sprig or two of fresh mint to the pan at this stage. Bring to the boil and simmer fast for about 10 minutes (for cannonballs; half that time for young or frozen peas), until the peas are completely tender.

Drain the peas, discarding the mint leaves if you have used any, but reserving the cooking liquor, and mash or process with a knob of butter, adding just enough of the liquor to give a loose but thick purée. You can make the purée as coarse or as smooth as you like. My preference is for velvety smooth – in contrast to my mushy peas (page 72). Taste and adjust the seasoning.

To serve, ladle generous pools of the purée on to warmed plates and lay thick slices of the ham or bacon on top.

- -

Garlic, salt and pepper prawns

This is what I do with the prawns I catch myself in Dorset, from mid-August until November (at which point the stormy seas tend to suggest my little boat would be better out of the harbour and in the boatyard for a winter rest-up). You can make the dish with shell-on prawns, which are worth buying frozen in bulk and defrosting in batches as you need them (since that's exactly what the fishmonger does).

This dish is all about fingers, and the garlicky, oily, prawny taste that is left on them when you've peeled. So please don't make it with peeled prawns and please don't use a knife and fork. It just wouldn't be fun.

To serve 2 generously, 4 less so

Take **500g live prawns or thoroughly defrosted raw shell-on prawns**. The former should be dropped in well-salted boiling water for 1 minute, then removed with a slotted spoon and set aside.

Melt about **50g butter** in a large frying pan and add a trickle of **olive oil** to help prevent it burning. Add 2 finely chopped cloves of **garlic** and fry gently, so the garlic softens without browning. Turn up the heat and add the prawns. Toss and shake, coating them thoroughly with the garlic and butter. Sprinkle, as you go, with generous pinches of **flaky sea salt** and vigorous twists of freshly ground **black pepper**. About 2–3 minutes on a fierce heat should do it. The idea is to get the prawns thoroughly hot, but stop before they start to shrink and lose their juices.

Serve at once, with brown bread and no cutlery.

Young leeks vinaigrette

This is an old-fashioned and simple recipe that I include because, although we eat leeks by the ton, the dish that shows them at their youthful sweet and tender best rarely gets made.

To serve 4 as a starter

Trim and wash **12–16 young leeks**. Leave them whole, slicing part-way down the green tops to help you rinse out any grit. Steam or blanch the leeks for 6–8 minutes, until tender, then drain thoroughly and lay in a warmed dish in which they fit snugly in a single layer.

In a jam jar with a lid, shake together 1 good teaspoon **English mustard**, ½ teaspoon **sugar**, 1 tablespoon **cider vinegar or white wine vinegar**, 3 tablespoons **olive oil** and some **salt** and **black pepper** until thick and emulsified. Pour this dressing all over the leeks while they are still warm and leave them to cool in it, turning them occasionally so they are well coated. Serve with soft brown bread.

Sour cherry brownies

The short season for English cherries rarely extends beyond the end of August, and the season for the sour-sharp Morello, the best of all cooking cherries, is just about contained within the month. It's worth seeking them out, though, as they are very special. You can use other cherries for this dish, but taste before you buy and choose those that have at least some natural tartness, even if they are really dessert cherries.

The cherry–chocolate combination is perhaps best known in the classic Black Forest gâteau. This is a more homely version, which I actually rather prefer.

To make 12 brownies

Take **a kilo of Morello or other tart cherries**, de-stalked and washed, and slit them to the stone on one side. Don't try and remove the stone, but put the cherries in a pan with 3–4 tablespoons water and **100g caster sugar**. Cook over a low heat until the juices run, stir to dissolve the sugar, then simmer very gently until the cherries are tender. Lift them from the juices with a slotted spoon and set aside, then boil the syrup to reduce it to an intense, tart but sweet syrup. Remove from the heat and return the cherries to the pan.

Now make a batch of my ultimate double-chocolate brownies. Cream **125g soft unsalted butter** with **200g caster sugar**. Beat in **2 eggs**, then **50g unsweetened cocoa powder**. Melt **100g good dark cooking chocolate** with 2 tablespoons **warm milk** and beat that in too. Finally, fold in **75g self-raising flour**. Spread the batter evenly in a greased and lined baking tin, about 15 x 25cm and at least 2cm deep. Bake at 170°C/Gas Mark 3 for about 25–30 minutes, until a skewer inserted in the centre comes out slightly sticky. Remove from the oven and leave on a wire rack for a few minutes to cool slightly, but cut into squares while still warm.

Serve the warm brownies with the warm cherries and syrup spooned over and sinking in, and a scoop of good-quality vanilla or chocolate ice-cream on top of that. Don't worry if you think you've died and gone to heaven. This is a normal reaction.

feb   mar   apr   may   jun   jul   aug   sep   oct   nov   dec

SEPTEMBER _____

Roast tomato purée, becoming chilled tomato soup with pesto__[177]__Vichyssoise with oyster croûtons__[178] Tomato and bread salad__[180]____Cockles and mussels with smoked bacon and chard__[182]_____Sprats__[185] Glutney__[186]_____Blackberry, apple and almond cobbler__[188]_____Plum or damson jampote, with hot and sour dipping sauce by-product__[189]

For many years, September meant going back to school after the summer holidays. More often than not the return to uniform and class drudgery was carried out under the glare of a baking late-summer sun. Among other things, it made me yearn for beach cricket on wet sand rather than rugby on knee-grazing parched earth.

So I guess September was always going to take some forgiving. But it's only since I moved full time to Dorset that I've come to appreciate the month for what it can and should be, in a good year: the culmination of all summer's promises, and the atonement for a good many of its let-downs.

Perhaps I'm rhapsodising excessively. But I'm writing in October, and the September just past was an absolute humdinger. It rained somewhere around the 5th, but from then until the end of the month the sun just shone. The best news was that a light offshore breeze meant the sea was in good nick for boating all month. As in June, my lobster pots were hauled almost daily, and from mid-August my prawn pots were going in, too. So, throughout September, I had a starter-sized portion of prawns for the three of us on just about every haul (the picture on page 167 is of probably my smallest haul all summer!). A lot of undersized lobsters went back, but a couple of good 'uns continued to pop up every week, along with some good-sized brown crabs and spider crabs.

A quick troll off the back of the boat was sure to produce some fat mackerel. Curiously absent during August, they were now back with a vengeance, chasing the shoals of sprats, and anything that remotely resembled them, sometimes within a few metres of the beach.

But undoubtedly the fishy highlight of the month was going after the sprats themselves. On several September mornings I went down to West Bay to find the harbour packed with a massive, shifting shoal of silvery fishes. My boating and fishing buddy, Nick Fisher (real name), has a traditional throw net, and a few well-aimed chucks on top of the glinting pile would net us half a bucket in no time. One day I returned home after such a session and when I tipped my share of the catch into the sink it almost filled it. I felt I had been a bit too greedy. To assuage my guilt, I got on the phone and called up friends and neighbours for an impromptu sprat barbecue. Not a morsel was left, and I felt justice had been done.

The garden was, of course, competing for my time, being highly productive throughout the month. Although fishing usually won, I did manage to bottle enough chutney (or glutney, as I like to call it) to feed an army of ploughmen. Once this is done, you can relax about the on-going glut of vegetables and just continue to enjoy them when you feel like it. I have to admit that the pigs probably ate more courgettes, or at least marrows, than I did this September. Meanwhile, the seafood diet was variously accompanied by the continuing harvest of spinach, carrots, beetroot, artichokes, runner and French beans, Tuscan kale, romanesco broccoli, onions, rocket, fennel and chicory.

However, this glorious month had its lows as well as highs. If there's one creature that loves a warm, sunny September more than I do it's the cabbage white butterfly. I wasn't quick enough off the mark, and one row of purple sprouting broccoli was shredded before I could get my hands on the little bastards. The cabbage white caterpillars are voracious eaters. One day they are the size of grains of rice – dozens of them scarcely visible on the brassica leaves to whose undersides they cling. The next they are like wriggling green chipolatas, and the leaf that fattened them has become a green lace doily.

Once I'd cottoned on to the problem I showed no mercy. I garden organically, though, so chemical warfare was out of the question. Instead, daily sorties were made to the brassica beds and the caterpillars were picked off by hand. This leaves one with the rather grisly problem of disposal. Squashing hundreds of goo-filled caterpillars just seemed too revolting. So I'm afraid I got others to do my dirty work. I served them up on a cabbage leaf of a plate to my beloved chickens, who seemed very grateful indeed. It is pleasing that these pernicious larvae were not only spared a chemical fate but even made a contribution to my breakfast egg.

feb   mar   apr   may   jun   jul   aug   sep   oct   nov   dec

I didn't wage war on just the caterpillars. In my garden I'm afraid the sins of the sons are visited on the fathers – and indeed the mothers. A single cabbage white female lays thousands of eggs, which will quickly become hundreds of tiny caterpillars. So Oscar and some of his friends were recruited to help tackle the problem at source, becoming mercenary butterfly hunters. The reward was 10p a specimen – dead or alive. By the end of the month, Oscar's piggy bank had a very healthy rattle. The broccoli went on to stage a remarkable recovery, so our efforts were not in vain.

September is also a good month for killing a steer. They are in prime condition after a summer of fattening on the grass, so much so that they don't even need 'finishing' (traditionally many beef steers get a supplementary feed of rolled barley for a month or so before slaughter). There are bureaucratic reasons for killing at this time of year, too. Since the BSE outbreak, all cattle for beef must be slaughtered by 30 months of age. My cows are Devon Rubys (page 217 – lovely, aren't they?). They are one of the finest beef breeds there is (not that I'm biased) and a great West Country favourite. The trouble is, they are slow growers, and can't be forced – one of the reasons their meat is so good. Ideally they should be killed at three years or over. But until the legislation changes, the best we can do is take them as close as possible to the 30-month deadline. Like most low-maintenance extensive suckler herds, my cows generally calve outdoors in April or May, which means, 30 months later, they'll be ready for slaughter in September or October.

I hang my beef for a full month at the abattoir, and sometimes hang a forerib joint for a further two weeks in the cool, airy meat safe in our kitchen wall. I bring the carcass home to butcher it – with my old River Cottage pal, Ray Smith. It takes the best part of a day to do the job, and when we sit down for lunch everyone gets to eat their favourite steak. For me it's a sirloin, Marie and Oscar go for the rump, while Ray has been known to manage a T-bone.

Of course it's the best steak I've ever tasted. And it certainly makes a welcome change from all that fish!

Roast tomato purée, becoming chilled tomato soup with pesto

This rich purée is one of the best and simplest products of the tomato glut, and can be frozen in great quantities for use in soups, stews and pasta dishes through the winter and spring.

Turning the freshly made purée into a great summer soup is easy peasy, and the pesto garnish sharpens it up into something really special.

To serve 4

Slice about **2 kilos of good, ripe tomatoes** in half and place cut-side up on a baking tray in a single layer. Bruise and roughly chop **3–4 large garlic cloves** and scatter them over the tomatoes. Season well with **salt** and **pepper**, sprinkle with a pinch of **sugar** and trickle over a little **olive oil**. Roast in a moderate oven (180°C/Gas Mark 4) for about 45 minutes, until the tomatoes are well browned and beginning to ooze juice. Remove from the oven and leave to cool for a few moments. Place a sieve over a bowl and rub the tomatoes through it to extract all the juice and flesh. You can freeze the purée at this stage for all kinds of uses.

Making the soup is just a matter of fine-tuning the purée with stock and various seasonings. First it's worth deglazing the syrupy, sticky juices in the baking tray by stirring in a little hot **stock** (vegetable, chicken or beef) or water, then adding these juices to the sieved tomato pulp. Tomatoes vary in juiciness and flavour, so taste the mixture and adjust the seasonings as necessary. Thinning with a little more stock or water will help produce the flavour and consistency you want. You can adjust acidity and sweetness with a squeeze of **lemon** or another pinch of **sugar**.

When you're happy with the soup, place the bowl in the fridge and chill for at least 4 hours (or place the bowl in a larger bowl of ice and water and stir occasionally).

For the pesto, pound or chop together a good fistful of **basil**, a clove of **garlic** and a handful of lightly pan-toasted **pine nuts**, until you have a fine-grained pulp. Stir in 2 tablespoons **olive oil**. You can add 1–2 tablespoons freshly grated **Parmesan** if you like. Leaving it to stand for an hour or two will help mellow the harsh edge of the raw garlic.

To serve the soup, ladle it into chilled bowls and trickle a generous tablespoon of the pesto over each portion.

feb   mar   apr   may   jun   jul   aug   sep   oct   nov   dec

Vichyssoise with oyster croûtons

Traditionally British native oysters come back into season in September – the first month with an 'r' in it since April. In fact, the widespread farming of Portuguese or 'rock' oysters, which remain safely edible throughout the summer months (though they go a bit 'milky', which is not to everyone's taste), means that oysters are now available all year round. But I still think it's nice to mark the moment, and with native oysters if you can afford them.

I love this dish. I had a hunch that oysters would go well with Vichyssoise and when I put it to the test I was delighted. I don't do much 'fancy' cooking but this is a very elegant dish, and yet it's easy to make – the hardest part being shucking the oysters, which I can rarely do without injuring myself.

This is September, and you can serve the soup chilled with raw oysters or hot with poached ones, depending on your mood and the weather.

To serve 5 – 6

Peel about **500g floury potatoes** and cut them into large chunks. Rinse well. Clean and slice **3–4 leeks**, discarding the very green ends. Melt **50g butter** in a large pan, add the leeks and sweat until soft. Add the potatoes and cover with **1 litre chicken, vegetable or fish stock**. Bring to the boil and simmer until the potatoes are completely tender. Remove the potatoes with a slotted spoon and rub them through a sieve (better than blending them, which can make the soup gluey). Purée the leeks in a blender with a little of the stock from the pan and a good pinch of **curry powder**.

Put the sieved potatoes in a clean pan, add the puréed leeks and the rest of the stock, plus 2 tablespoons **double cream**. Mix well with a whisk so the soup is well blended and velvety smooth. If it seems a little thick, thin with some more hot stock or milk. Check and adjust the seasoning, which should be a little more emphatic if you are planning to serve the soup chilled.

To serve chilled

Leave the soup in the fridge, or in a bowl over iced water, until thoroughly chilled. Shuck **up to 3 fresh, live oysters per person**, depending on budget and the size of the oysters.

Lightly **butter** some thin slices of **brown bread** and, using a pastry cutter, stamp into little oyster-sized rounds or ovals. Season with a twist of **pepper** and place an oyster on each one. Ladle the chilled soup into bowls and carefully lay the oyster bread boats on the surface of the soup. For an optional, but worthwhile and very pretty, garnish, thin **100ml crème fraîche** with a squeeze of **lemon juice** and stir in some finely chopped **chives or chervil**. Spoon a teaspoon of this mixture over each oyster.

To serve hot

Stamp out little rounds of **white or brown bread** and fry them gently in **oil or clarified butter** until golden brown. Set aside, keeping them warm.

Next steam open the oysters: in a wide pan with a lid, bring **a large glass of wine**, a large glass of water and a knob of **butter** to the boil. Add **up to 3 unshucked oysters per person** and replace the lid. Leave for just 2 minutes, then take the pan off the heat and remove the oysters. The shells should have opened a fraction. Open them up and carefully remove the poached oysters whole, pouring any juices back into the pan. You can, if you like, make a little sauce from these winey juices: strain them into a clean pan through a cloth and boil until reduced to about 2–3 tablespoonfuls. Then add 1 tablespoon **double cream**. Bubble until thick and glossy, take off the heat and stir in 1 tablespoon finely chopped **chives and/or chervil**.

Reheat the soup thoroughly, without quite boiling, just before serving. Ladle the hot soup into warmed bowls. Place each warm poached oyster on a fried bread croûton and float the croûtons on top of the soup. Spoon a little of the creamy sauce over each oyster and garnish with a scattering of chopped chives or chervil. Serve at once.

To eat

Don't be shy. Unless the oysters are enormous, I would pick up a whole oyster croûton and eat it in one go, have a few spoonfuls of soup and then tackle another croûton. Really big oysters might require two bites at the croûton.

feb   mar   apr   may   jun   jul   aug   sep   oct   nov   dec

Tomato and bread salad

This is a version of the classic Italian dish, *panzanella*, where the ripest possible tomatoes are tossed with stale bread, olive oil and various other goodies. For me it's a way of celebrating my best, juiciest slicing tomatoes, which usually come good in the polytunnel early this month – varieties such as Big Boy, Marmande and the superb Italian ones, Cuor di Bue (Ox Heart) and Costoluto Fiorentino, available from Franchi Sementi (tel: 020 8930 2516). Hence the 'pizza style' presentation, with the various components scattered over a base of luscious tomato slices.

To serve 4

Choose **a kilo of the ripest, tastiest slicing tomatoes** you can get. Slice them horizontally, about ½–1cm thick, discarding just the coarse, stalky slice from the top. Cover 4 plates with slightly overlapping slices of tomato. Season sparingly with **flaky salt** and freshly ground **black pepper**, then less sparingly with a trickle of **good olive oil**.

Tear up 4 thick slices of slightly stale **coarse country bread**. Open **a small tin of anchovies in olive oil** and toss the bread with the oil from the tin, another tablespoon or so of **good olive oil** and a sprinkling of **good aged vinegar**, such as balsamic. Leave to macerate for at least half an hour, tossing again every few minutes. Meanwhile, separate the anchovies and slice them in half lengthways, if you like. Slice **1 large red onion** very finely and separate the slivers with your fingers. Stone a couple of dozen **black olives**. Take about 1 tablespoon **capers** and drain off the vinegar. Tear up at least a dozen **basil leaves**.

Scatter all these ingredients over the sliced tomatoes, dividing them roughly equally between the 4 plates. (Can you resist the temptation to customise your own plate, with more of the things you like most on it? I can't.)

Cockles and mussels with smoked bacon and chard

September is a good month for most shellfish, and mussels are at their peak from now until Christmas. Cockles are good, too, and although you can use either in this hearty shellfish soup, the combination of both is particularly winning. You can omit the bacon to make a very satisfactory meat-free version, but I am a sucker for that pork–shellfish marriage.

To serve 4 – 6 as a main course, 10 – 12 as a starter

Scrub and rinse **a kilo each of live cockles and mussels**, discarding any that don't close when handled. Roughly chop **1 onion**, bash, peel and roughly chop **2–3 garlic cloves** and sweat them in **50g butter** and 1 tablespoon **oil** in a large pan.

After a couple of minutes, and before either garlic or onion start to colour, add **1 large glass of white wine** (about a third of a bottle) and the same amount of water. Bring to a rapid boil and add about a fifth to a third of the shellfish, depending on the size of the pan (you should cook in batches no more than 2–3 shells deep). Put the lid on, give the pan a shake or a stir after 1 minute and check after 2. After no more than 3 minutes, almost all the shells should be open. Remove the shellfish with a slotted spoon, transferring them to a colander over a deep dish where the rest of their juices can collect. Any cockles or mussels that have failed to open can be put back in the pan for another minute, but if that doesn't do it, then discard them.

Cook the remaining shellfish in the same way, then strain the liquor from both the pan and the dish – first through a sieve, then through muslin or cotton – to remove any fine grit. I like to have some shells in this soup, so I usually remove only half to two-thirds of the cockles and mussels from their shells. Whatever you like.

To finish the dish, cut **250g thickly sliced smoked bacon or smoked pancetta** into 2cm strips. Cut out the thick white stems from **500g Swiss chard** and slice these into 5cm lengths. Shred the green leaves quite finely. Heat a film of **olive oil** in a large saucepan and fry the bacon until almost crisp. Pour in the strained cooking liquor from the shellfish, then taste and check the seasoning. It will be salty, but that's the way of this dish. If it's very salty,

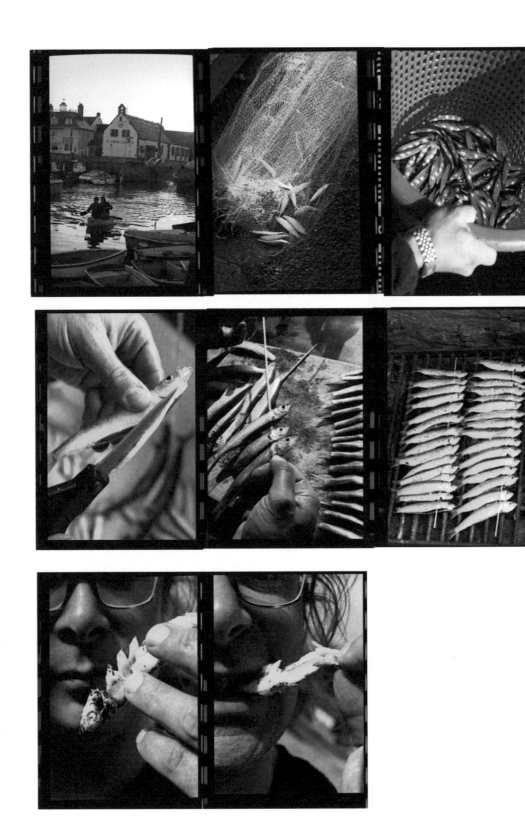

add a little water, but not too much or you'll dilute the lovely fishy flavours (if you happen to have some good, unsalted fish or chicken **stock**, you could add that).

Bring the liquor to the boil and add the sliced chard stems. About 3 minutes later, add the shredded leaves. A minute after that, return all the cockles and mussels to the pan, mix well, and a minute later serve it all up, in warmed bowls.

- -

Sprats

Sprats must be one of the most under-appreciated delights of the English marine harvest. Here in Dorset, though, a fair few of us have cottoned on. At some point before the end of September, and thereafter several times in October and November, huge shoals of sprats will amass off the coast, harried in by the mackerel and sea birds. Sometimes the waves of the big spring tides will dump them, live and wriggling, right on the shingle of the beach, and those lucky enough to be around will fill their pockets, bags and even – quite literally – boots. The sprats also swarm into the harbour sometimes, where, as you can see from the pictures opposite, a drop net or throw net can be used to haul them by the dozen.

The resulting feast is always a joy. You don't really have to gut them when they're this fresh; I usually just snip the belly and the gills so that everything can be eaten. And then I lay them on lightly oiled foil, season with salt and pepper and flash them under a very hot grill so they blister and crackle. Turned after 3 minutes, they're done in 5. Or, in barbecue weather, I'll fire up the charcoal, thread the sprats in batches of 15 or 20 through the head on to a bamboo skewer (see opposite), brush with oil and grill them on the fire.

They don't need much – sometimes just a squeeze of lemon, sometimes a little dipping sauce made of mustard, crème fraîche and a pinch of sugar. This year I tried them with my home-made plum dipping sauce (page 189). Wonderful.

- -

feb   mar   apr   may   jun   jul   aug   sep   oct   nov   dec

Glutney

This is a 'multiple choice' recipe for chutney, designed to help you use whatever seasonal fruit and vegetables are in full glut at the time. For me, the courgettes/overgrown marrows are pretty much a staple in August and September, and they may give way to pumpkins and squashes in October and November. Tomatoes and plums are around at roughly the same time, though the tomatoes will start early – particularly if you use green ones.

Of course, no two batches of glutney will ever be quite the same – but that hardly matters. You should also feel free to play fast and loose with the spice bag. And if you like a really hot chutney, add as much dried chilli as you dare.

Serve with cheese, cold meats, terrines, pork pies etc. But also remember what a useful ingredient chutney is, with a ready-mixed blend of sweet, sour and spice. I frequently add it to curries, soups and stews.

To make about 10 jam jars' worth

You will need either **a kilo of marrows/overgrown courgettes or a kilo of pumpkin**, plus either **a kilo of red or green tomatoes, or a kilo of plums**. Marrows or courgettes should be unpeeled but cut into dice no bigger than 1cm (discard seeds from really large marrows), while pumpkin should be peeled, seeds and soft fibres discarded, and similarly diced. Tomatoes should be scalded, skinned and roughly chopped, while plums just need stoning and chopping. Peel and dice about **1 kilo cooking or eating apples** and **500g onions**. Put the vegetables and fruit in a large, heavy-based pan with **500g sultanas or raisins, 500g light brown sugar, 750ml white wine or cider vinegar,** made up to 1 litre with water, 1–3 teaspoons **dried chilli flakes**, depending on your taste for heat, and 1 teaspoon **salt**.

Make up a spice bag by tying in a square of muslin or cotton a thumb-sized nugget of **fresh or dried ginger**, roughly chopped, a dozen **cloves**, around a dozen **black peppercorns**, a generous teaspoon of **coriander seeds** and a few blades of **mace**. Add the spice bag to the pan, pushing it into the middle.

Heat the mixture gently, stirring occasionally to dissolve the sugar, and bring slowly to the boil. Simmer for 2–3 hours, uncovered, stirring regularly to ensure it does not burn on the

bottom of the pan. The chutney is ready when it is rich, thick and reduced, and parts to reveal the base of the pan when a wooden spoon is dragged through it. If it starts to dry out before this stage is reached, add a little boiling water.

Pot up the chutney while still warm (but not boiling hot) in sterilised jars with plastic-coated screw-top lids (essential to stop the vinegar interacting with the metal). Leave to mature for at least 2 weeks – ideally 2 months – before serving.

- -

Blackberry, apple and almond cobbler

The cobbler is a classic English pudding – a close cousin of the crumble, yet for some inexplicable reason not as well known. It's hardly any more time-consuming to make, and the crusty, scone-like topping is quite wonderful.

Blackberry and apple is a traditional late-summer filling, as the last of the blackberries overlap with the first of the cooking apples, such as Grenadier. It's worth freezing plenty of blackberries to use when the Bramleys are at their best.

This cobbler can easily be adapted for all kinds of fruit – plums and damsons now, rhubarb and gooseberries earlier in the summer. Just slightly sweeten the fruit and cook to a juicy compote, then pile the cobblers on top and bake.

To serve 6

Peel, core and slice about **1 kilo of Bramleys or other dissolving cooking apples**. Put into a saucepan with about **100g sugar**, a small knob of **butter** and a couple of tablespoons of water. Heat very gently until the juices begin to run. Cook the apples at a very gentle simmer for about 15 minutes, stirring occasionally, until you have a smooth compote. Taste for sweetness and add more sugar if you like, but keep it on the tart side. Then stir in about **500g blackberries** and pile the mixture into a pie dish or other ovenproof dish, leaving a good couple of centimetres spare at the top.

Now make the cobbler topping. Mix **100ml whole milk**, slightly warmed, with 1 teaspoon **lemon juice** and set aside. Sift **100g plain flour** and 1 tablespoon **baking powder** into a bowl and rub in **75g butter** until you have fine crumbs. Stir in **100g ground almonds** and **50g caster sugar**, then mix in the milk to give a soft dough. You can do all this in a food processor, pulsing first the flour, baking powder and butter, then the almonds and sugar, then the milk.

Pile generous dessertspoons of the mixture (each one a 'cobbler' not quite touching its neighbour) over the surface of the fruit in the dish. Aim for 6–8 cobblers in all. Scatter over 1 tablespoon **flaked almonds**, if you like. Place the dish in the centre of a moderate oven (180°C/Gas Mark 4) and bake for about 30 minutes, until the cobblers are puffed and golden, like crusty scones. Leave to cool for 15 minutes or so (otherwise it will be scalding hot when you serve it). Serve plain, or with cream, custard or ice-cream.

Note

If you want to part-make the pudding a few hours in advance, prepare the fruit compote and mix the cobbler ingredients up to the point where you add the milk. Then about 45 minutes before you want to eat it (just before you sit down to lunch or dinner) whisk in the warm milk, make the cobblers, and put in the oven.

- -

Plum or damson jampote, with hot and sour dipping sauce by-product

I love plum jam and I love plum compote, and I particularly love this dish, which ends up somewhere between the two – hence the name. It can be used as a sauce for vanilla ice-cream or a topping for pancakes, or like a runny jam for spreading on scones, toast and pikelets (page 225). It's excellent trickled on rice pudding, and even porridge! It also makes the wonderfully simple pudding you see in the picture on page 191, chilled with yoghurt and custard. It's one of my favourite pictures, and puddings, in the whole book.

As if that wasn't reason enough to give it a whirl, you also get, at no extra charge and little extra effort, a bottle or two of my hot and sour plum sauce. This makes a superb dipping sauce for all kinds of crispy fried or grilled food, particularly pork, poultry (especially duck, of course), prawns and squid. I love serving it with grilled sprats (page 185) and it's even rather good trickled on cheese on toast.

Choose small, firm, sour cooking plums, or even damsons, rather than the big, watery eaters. They have more natural pectin, which makes for a good syrup, and they should keep a little bit of shape, even after hard boiling.

For every **kilo of plums** you will need **500g caster sugar**. Put the whole plums and the sugar in a large, heavy-based pan with enough water to come halfway up the plums. Heat gently, stirring to dissolve the sugar. Simmer for 15–20 minutes, until the plums are tender, then strain off about 500ml of the syrupy juice through a sieve into a clean pan.

Attend to this syrup, which will make your hot and sour dipping sauce, while the pan of plums cools down a bit. Add to the syrup **1–2 garlic cloves**, very finely chopped, **1–2 small hot chillies**, fresh if possible, deseeded and very finely chopped, **100ml light soy sauce** and **100ml brown rice vinegar or good cider vinegar**. Stir well and bring to the boil, then boil rapidly over a high heat for about 5 minutes (keep your nose away from the powerful vinegar fumes!). While still hot, pour through a clean funnel into 1 large or 2 or 3 smaller sterilised bottles, ideally screw-top. The sauce should keep for up to a year in a fridge.

To finish the plums, work through the mixture when it is cool enough to handle, lifting the plums out with a large spoon, removing the stones, and some of the skins if you like, then transferring them to a clean bowl. Return the sorted, stoneless compote to the pan, bring back to the boil and boil hard for about 5 minutes to give a thick, pulpy compote, which is on its way to being a jam. This is not as reliable a keeper as a regular jam, and may eventually start to ferment. But it will keep for up to 3 months in the fridge.

It's endlessly versatile, as discussed above. For a really wonderful pudding, serve with equal quantities of cold fresh egg custard and unsweetened yoghurt: pile them separately into a bowl, then 'dabble' with your spoon, varying the combination in each mouthful, till you stir it all up into a gorgeous, swirly mess of a fool.

OCTOBER_____

When the leaves are still turning from green to yellow (which is usually the case at the beginning of October), then as long as the weather is fine you can continue to persuade yourself that it is summer. But when the leaves are unambiguously brown, and there are almost as many of them on the ground as on the trees (which is *always* the case by the end of October), then it's time to face facts: summer's over. That's okay, though – because now you can concentrate on the many culinary delights of autumn.

If you weren't already on the case in mid-September, then it's time to get out the woolly socks and garters, along with the cleft walking stick and leather hat. (You don't have to dress like an idiot when mushroom hunting but a lot of people seem to think it helps.)

You certainly don't need to live in the country to forage for fungi. Urban enthusiasts should be on the alert, too. Many of our parks and play areas have grass and wooded areas that are unsprayed and ungrazed and therefore prime habitat for wild-mushroom hunting. Hyde Park in central London has been known to yield some monster puffballs. Hampstead Heath and Epping Forest are also teeming with edible varieties. No doubt urban parks across the UK can yield similar finds. Even the rural mycophile should be 'urban aware'. I have found a good crop of parasol mushrooms growing on a roundabout on the outskirts of Bridport.

Don't take any chances when collecting fungi. A comprehensive field guide, such as Roger Phillips' *Mushrooms and Other Fungi of Great Britain and Europe* (Pan Books, 1981), is invaluable. You should never risk eating a mushroom unless you are completely confident of its identification. There are some virulently poisonous fungi out there, so there's not mushroom for error (sorry).

Incidentally, we may be in the October chapter but it's worth noting that the season for gathering mushrooms is far longer than many amateur enthusiasts generally give credit for. Many varieties – notably chanterelles and field mushrooms – are a summer phenomenon as much as an autumn one. And when autumn is preferred (as with hedgehog fungus and wood blewits, for example), the very mild weather of recent years has meant good hauls can be had as late as early December.

Your forest foraging may also lead you to some other October treats: sloes, crab apples and the first of the sweet chestnuts. British chestnuts gathered from the wild may be smaller than those imported from the Continent but they have at least as good a flavour. If you find a windfall, it's worth filling your boots, as they keep well too. Let them dry in a warm room for a day or so, then store them in a cool, dry place and they'll keep until Christmas.

And, of course, it would be criminal not to make the most of our native apples and pears. I have chosen six varieties of apple for my little orchard, with two trees of each variety. I can tell you, I agonised over the catalogue (from Scott's of Merriot, which is luckily just a few miles away in Somerset). My aim was to get a range of delicious, characterful apples, favouring those that are crisp and tart over ones that may be sweeter and softer (that's my personal taste). I also wanted a crop that spreads through the season, in both directions, from its prime in October. I had the catalogue in bed for weeks. But in the end I think I did pretty well. Here's what I plumped for, in cropping order:

D i s c o v e r y The first to ripen, these can usually be picked by mid-August. Crisp and juicy, tart and refreshing, though relatively 'one-note' in flavour. Discovery are useless keepers and are best eaten straight from the tree. They are all over by the beginning of October.

G r e n a d i e r A very useful early cropper, this is technically a cooker. However, thin slices of the tart, crisp flesh have a fresh, summery taste and go very well in a salad or with cheese. They also make a delicious, tart juice that can be sweetened with a little icing sugar and frozen as a granita or sorbet.

B r a m l e y ' s   S e e d l i n g The ultimate cooker, Bramleys cook naturally and quickly to a tart, refreshing pulp, which is the basis of all the best apple pies and crumbles, as well as my Bramley burnt creams (page 227). Usually ready to pick by the end of October, they are really a November apple. If you wrap them individually in newspaper and store in a cool place, they will keep right through the winter until March.

Egremont Russet Though a few people seem mildly phobic about its rough, russeted skin, this apple is widely loved, and rightly so. It has to be the ultimate 'nutty' apple. Crisp and sweet, it is very hard to beat for flavour. Personally I prefer it towards the beginning of the season (October), when it has more crispness and acidity, but others go the opposite way, admiring the fully rounded flavour of apples that have been in store for a while. As this implies, it is a reasonable keeper – but not much cop after Christmas.

Ashmead's Kernel An outstanding late apple, which is not usually ready until mid-November. It has a brilliant crisp texture and delightful, almost sherbety taste, with an excellent balance of fruit flavours, sweetness and acidity. Sadly they are not very productive. My two-year-old tree produced only two fruits last year!

Orleans Reinette Another late apple, this is fortunately hardier and more prolific than Ashmead's Kernel, which, with its slight russeting and pinky-orange bloom, it closely resembles. But it doesn't keep as well. Apart from that, I can't recommend this underrated apple highly enough. It has a wonderfully complex flavour, which combines the Russet's mellowness and nuttiness with Ashmead's lively sparkle, and even some tropical, lychee-like overtones.

Of course, this is a highly personal selection. There are dozens of other English varieties that I could have gone for, and would probably now love just as much. As a matter of principle, I taste and buy every new English apple I encounter during the season. With this kind of exploratory tasting in mind, October is a great month for visiting farmers' markets. You may well discover a new personal favourite, and perhaps even feel moved to grow it.

Incidentally, we are generally very bad at keeping our apples at home. Almost any apple left in the fruit bowl in a warm kitchen will go into rapid decline, getting wrinkly on the outside and soft and mealy inside. Apples should be kept in a cool larder or even the fridge, and they will remain the outstanding seasonal treats that they ought to be.

Roast pumpkin (or squash) soup

I've always liked pumpkins and squashes made into a soup, and I love them roasted, too. This year, thinking how delicious the flavours are that you get when you roast peppers and tomatoes, and what good soup they make, I decided on a similar approach with my favourite squash varieties. The result was gorgeous. You can use any pumpkin or squash for this soup, and the ever-popular butternut works particularly well. But if you can get (or grow) some of the other sweet squash varieties, such as Sweet Mama, Blue Kuri, Sweet Dumpling, Crown Prince or Table Ace, generally available from mid-October to late November, then so much the better.

To serve 4

Take **1 medium pumpkin or 2 small squashes**. There's no need to peel them. Just cut them into rough chunks or thick slices and scrape away the pips and surrounding soft fibres. Lay the pieces in a large roasting tin and generously trickle over them up to 2 tablespoons **olive oil**. Scatter half a dozen **garlic cloves**, whole, with the skin on, but lightly crushed, over the roasting tin and season well with **salt** and **black pepper**.

Put in a fairly hot oven (190°C/Gas Mark 5) for 35–40 minutes, turning once or twice if you like, until the pumpkin pieces are tender and nicely browned. Use a spoon to scrape the soft flesh away from the skin.

Heat **1 litre chicken or vegetable stock** in a large pan. Squeeze out the flesh from the roasted garlic cloves and put it in a liquidiser with the pumpkin flesh and enough hot stock to cover it (do this in batches). Liquidise until completely smooth, then pour into a clean pan. Taste the soup and adjust the seasoning. Add more stock to adjust the consistency – I think it should be pretty thick and creamy.

Heat the soup through without letting it boil. Meanwhile, fry a few slivers of **garlic** in a little **oil**. Scatter the thin shards of crisp fried garlic over each bowl of hot soup as you serve it. Finish, if you like, with a trickle of olive oil or, better still, the delicious (and, I suspect, soon to be fashionable) Moroccan argan oil.

- -

feb   mar   apr   may   jun   jul   aug   sep   oct   nov   dec

Mixed wild mushrooms on toast

Gathering wild mushrooms is a haphazard business. Great fun, but of course you never know what you're going to end up with. The mixed bag in the picture was the result of scrabbling around nearby woods and hedges for a couple of hours on a late-October afternoon. The haul is mainly *Agaricus* types (relatives of the common field mushroom), especially horse mushrooms, plus a fair few wood blewits and parasols, a handful of chanterelles, and one tiny, thumb-sized cep. Nothing spectacular, but a tasty enough collection nonetheless.

I don't see the point of elaborate mushroom recipes. On the all too rare occasions when I have a fine haul of really fresh ceps, I may make Mauro Bregoli's superb cep lasagne, which you'll find in *The River Cottage Cookbook*. Otherwise, I know of no more suitable celebration of their freshness and intensity than simply frying them up in a little olive oil or bacon fat and serving them on toast. If I've really lucked out, and I still have an excess of fresh 'shrooms on hand, I'll make, and sometimes freeze, the soup that is the next recipe.

To serve 4

Sort through up to a kilo of positively identified edible **mixed wild mushrooms**, brushing away dirt and grit, trimming and discarding dodgy bits. Slice the larger ones, halve or quarter the smaller ones and leave any really tiny ones whole. Melt a good tablespoon of **bacon fat or olive oil** in a large frying pan and sweat 1–2 finely chopped cloves of **garlic** in it for a minute or so. Before the garlic takes colour, add the mushrooms. Fry gently at first, then turn up the heat as the juices run. Season with a little **salt** and **pepper** early on and throw in a couple of sprigs of **fresh thyme or** a good pinch of **dried thyme**. Continue to cook until the watery juices have run out and mostly evaporated (depending on the type of mushrooms and their condition, the amount of liquid may be considerable). Taste and check for seasoning. A tiny squeeze of **lemon juice** and a modest pinch of **cayenne pepper** can work wonders. And a scattering of finely chopped **parsley** is equally optional but usually, I think, desirable.

Make some **toast** (I greedily chose the top of a whole loaf for my dish in the picture) and, if you like, rub it lightly with a clove of raw garlic before either buttering it or drizzling it with a little olive oil. Pile the hot mushrooms on the hot toast and eat at once.

Mushroom soup

A home-made wild mushroom soup is not encountered often enough but when it is, it is invariably a tremendous treat.

To serve 4

Take about a kilo of **mixed wild mushrooms** and proceed precisely as in the recipe above to the end of the first paragraph (including the **lemon juice**, **cayenne** and **parsley**). You don't have to cook out quite so much of the liquid though.

Instead of making toast, put the mushrooms in a liquidiser with **600ml hot stock**, a good knob of **butter** and 1 heaped tablespoon **cooked long grain rice or a couple of rice cakes**. (This is an excellent way of thickening soups to velvety smoothness, with none of the glueyness you can get when processing cooked potatoes.) Blend until smooth, but still speckled with tiny mushroom pieces. Pour into a saucepan and heat through, adding more stock to thin it to the consistency you prefer and stirring in a spoonful of **cream** if you like. Taste and adjust the seasoning. A little splash of **dry sherry** can also be nice, but don't overdo it.

Now make toast, and serve it with the piping-hot soup.

Warm borlotti bean salad

By October the borlotti bean pods are showing their stunning red- and yellow-flecked colour and are full to bursting with beautiful variegated beans. When boiled, they have a mild flavour and a pleasant, creamy texture. In my garden the crop is bolstered by various overgrown varieties of French bean – especially Blue Lake and Cosi Violetti, one of the deep-purple varieties, whose leathery, semi-dried pods can now be plundered for the beans inside. All the beans are suitable for this simple treatment. You could also use dried borlotti or cannellini beans, soaked overnight and then boiled until tender.

To serve 4

Simmer about **500g fresh borlotti or other podded beans** in lightly salted water for 15–30 minutes (according to size and how dried out they are), until completely tender. While they are cooking, finely chop **a small onion** and combine with a few sprigs of finely chopped **parsley and/or coriander, a couple of large tomatoes**, skinned, deseeded and chopped, and a good tablespoon of **olive oil**. As soon as the beans are cooked, drain well, then toss with the rest of the ingredients while still hot. Serve warm.

- -

Flatbread stack with roasted peppers and borlotti beans

I love to grow a few varieties of chilli alongside the tomatoes in my polytunnel. My favourites are the peppy but not too lethal Hungarian hot wax and the rich and chocolatey poblano.

Though I may get a few in September, most of them come good in October, around the same time as the borlotti beans are ready for podding. I combine the two in various ways, sometimes just mixing roasted peeled chillies with cold boiled beans and a few trickles of good olive oil. But these 'sandwiches', which use a wonderfully simple flatbread that everyone should know how to make, are simply divine.

Once you've got the knack of making the bread, basically a simple pizza dough, you can use it in all kinds of ways at any time of year: a Taleggio, Parma ham and rocket melt was one recent invention that went down a storm. Fresh tomatoes, mozzarella and basil are good on a plate, but even better on an edible plate. There's no end to the possibilities . . .

To serve 4 as a supper sandwich, 8 as a starter

First make the dough for the flatbread. Mix 2 level teaspoons **dried yeast** with 200ml tepid water and leave for 5 minutes. Then top up with 100ml tepid water. Add to **500g strong**

white bread flour, with a good pinch of **salt** and 2 tablespoons **olive oil**. Mix to a firm dough. Turn out on to a lightly floured surface and knead thoroughly for a good 10 minutes, until smooth and elastic. Then place in a bowl, cover with a damp cloth and leave in a warm place for about 45 minutes or until roughly doubled in volume.

While the dough's doing its thing, take around **a dozen red peppers or fleshy mild chillies**, or better still a mixture, and put them in a roasting tin. Place in a fairly hot oven (190°C/Gas Mark 5) for about 25–30 minutes. They should be pretty well charred, but turn them and give them another 10 minutes if necessary. Place in a bowl, cover and leave until cool enough to handle. Carefully peel off the charred skin with your fingers, discarding it along with the seeds and stalks. Cut the peppers into strips and set aside.

Prepare a batch of the warm bean salad described on page 202, using about **250g borlotti or other fresh beans**. Or you can use dried or tinned beans, similarly dressed.

When the dough has risen, knock it back down, knead lightly and divide into 8 pieces. On a floured surface, roll them out to about 2mm thick. Heat a large, heavy frying pan or flat griddle until very hot. Lay a flatbread on the pan. After a minute or so, bubbles will start to form on the surface. Prick them. After 2–3 minutes, check the underside and, when it is lightly speckled with brown, turn it over. Another minute will brown the other side and finish the bread. Stack the flatbreads as they are ready, and cover with a cloth.

You need 3 flatbreads for each of 2 sandwiches (so you'll have 2 left over). Place the first flatbread on a baking sheet and spread half the borlotti bean mixture evenly over it. Place another flatbread on top and arrange half the strips of roasted peppers on it. Cut **250g goat's cheese log** into slices. Arrange half the cheese over the peppers, season well with **salt** and **black pepper** and trickle over a little **olive oil**. Place the third flatbread on top and trickle again. Construct a second sandwich in the same way, using 3 more flatbreads.

Place the baking tray with the 2 sandwiches in a hot oven (200°C/Gas Mark 6) for about 10 minutes, until they are heated through and the cheese is melting. Slice each sandwich in half, for 4 giant supper-sized sandwiches, or into quarters to give 8 starter-sized portions. Eat straight away, while hot and melty.

Note that the flatbreads don't keep well, but stale (day-old) ones can be baked until completely crisp, when they are very good for dipping or eating with cheese.

feb   mar   apr   may   jun   jul   aug   sep   oct   nov   dec

Poached pears with panna cotta and granita

You can poach a pear, and you can make panna cotta, and you can make a granita, and in all three cases you will have made a very fine and worthwhile dessert. But put them all together and you are into an irresistible exploration of taste, temperature and texture.

To serve 4

Take **4 good pears**, such as Conference or Comice; they may be firm or almost ripe, but should not be overripe. Peel them and place in a pan into which they fit fairly snugly. Pour in enough **white wine** (up to half a bottle) to cover them by three-quarters, add the juice of ½ **lemon** and **1 orange**, and top up with water to cover completely. Add to the pan a **cinnamon stick**, a few **peppercorns**, 3 or 4 **cloves**, a few strips of **lemon zest** and **50g caster sugar**. Bring gently to the boil, stirring occasionally to dissolve the sugar. Simmer until the pears are tender but not too soft. The time will depend on their ripeness: from 10 minutes to about 30.

Remove from the heat and leave to cool, then lift out the pears and put them in a polythene bag with a tablespoon of the cooking liquor. Keep in the fridge. Strain the rest of the liquor, discarding the spices and peels, and taste it. It should be tart and sweet, tasting of pear, spice and wine. Adjust with more lemon juice and more sugar only if you think it needs it. Then freeze in a Tupperware box. It's going to be your granita.

To make the panna cotta, split **1 vanilla pod** open lengthways and put it in a pan with **750ml single cream, or 500ml double cream plus 250ml whole milk**. Bring just to the boil, then remove from the heat. Soak 2 sheets of **leaf gelatine** in cold water for 5 minutes, then drain, gently squeezing out excess water. Stir the gelatine into the scalded cream, along with **25g caster sugar**. Scrape the seeds from the vanilla pod into the cream and discard the pod. Divide the cream between 4–5 small moulds, such as dariole moulds or ramekins, and put in the fridge to set.

When you serve up the dish, the pears should be at room temperature, the panna cotta at fridge temperature and the granita, of course, frozen – but remove it from the freezer about

30 minutes before serving. Place a pear on each plate. Wrap each panna cotta mould in a hot, damp cloth for about 10 seconds. Prod the edge with your finger to check it is released from the mould, then unmould directly on to the plate, beside the pear. Use a fork to scratch up the frozen liquor into frosty shards and pile a heap of this granita on the other side of the pear.

Serve at once, before anything melts, collapses or slides off the plate!

Autumn bliss

I worked this recipe out from scratch, experimenting with my kitchen collaborator, Bryan Johnson, and I have to say I couldn't be more delighted with the results. My plan was to celebrate the wonderful variety of autumn raspberry after which the dish is named. I wanted a dish that acknowledges the change in the weather, the creeping autumn chill, and therefore takes the raspberry away from its usual summer association of chilled desserts and into the realm of hot puddings.

It's really a three-way hybrid of English bread and butter pudding, French *pain perdu* and Italian ravioli! The only tricky bit is getting the seal tight round the edges of the squares of bread. I had to stop trying to do it with stale bread, which is what *pain perdu* ought to be made with, and use fresh. Then it's a doddle. Of course, once you've got the hang of it, you can fill this lovely pud with all sorts of seasonal goodies besides raspberries: Bramley apples, blackberries, plums, pears. But raspberries will prove hard to beat.

To serve 2

Start by making a simple raw custard. Beat **1 egg** and **1 extra egg yolk** with 1 tablespoon **caster sugar**, 2 tablespoons **single or double cream** and 3 tablespoons **milk**. Cut the crusts off 4 thick (1–2cm) slices of **fresh white bread** and spread a little soft **butter** in the middle of each (not to the edges, though, as it may prevent you making the seal). Take a couple of dozen **raspberries** and pile them into the centre of 2 slices (i.e. on top of the

butter), squashing them together a bit. Sprinkle a little **caster sugar** over them. Take the remaining 2 slices of bread and place them, buttered-side down, over the first. Squeeze the edges of the bread together firmly, making a seal all round the edges – you can use a little of the egg custard, dabbed on with a finger, to help it stick. You end up with a bread 'cushion', like a giant raviolo, in which the raspberries are the stuffing.

Pour the custard mixture into a shallow dish or deep plate and lay the bread cushions in it to soak up the custard. Turn them several times, until well saturated. Heat a good centimetre of untainted fresh **oil**, such as groundnut or sunflower oil, in a frying pan. When it is hot enough to turn a test piece of bread golden in about a minute, lift the eggy cushions with a spatula and slide them carefully into the pan. When the underneath is fried to a deep golden brown, turn them over and fry till the other side is done too.

Drain on kitchen paper, then transfer quickly to warmed plates. Dust with a little more caster sugar and serve piping hot.

Quince cheese

Making preserves isn't everyone's idea of fun. To be honest, it used not to be mine. But it turns out to be easier than you might think, and the end products are often extremely rewarding. This is a good project for a rainy afternoon – a commodity with which October can be unfailingly generous.

A 'cheese' is a fruit preserve so intensely reduced that it sets to an almost solid, fudge-like consistency that can be cut with a knife. Perhaps the best of all fruit cheeses, widely celebrated in Spain and Portugal as *membrillo*, is made from quinces. It comes into its own when served with the other kind of cheese, traditionally the strong and salty Iberian types usually made from sheep's and goat's milk. But it's every bit as good with a tangy piece of mature Cheddar, and with blue cheeses such as Stilton, Roquefort, and our own very fine Dorset Blue Vinney, too.

To make about 1.5 kg

Dissolve **1 kilo sugar** in 750ml water in a heavy pan over a low heat. Bring to the boil and boil hard for about 5 minutes to make a light syrup. Peel and core **3–4 large quinces**, about 1 kilo in all. Grate, mince or very finely chop the flesh, add to the syrup and bring back to the boil, stirring well. Simmer over a low heat, stirring regularly with a wooden spoon and taking care the mixture doesn't catch on the bottom of the pan, until reduced to a thick, grainy paste. It is ready when the spoon, dragged across the bottom of the pan, separates the paste, showing the clean bottom of the pan – this may take up to an hour.

Spread the cheese into lightly greased shallow dishes or trays and place in the lowest possible oven for 3–4 hours to harden further. Sometimes a light, sugary crust will form on the top – this is normal. Remove from the oven and leave to cool completely.

Don't store long term in metallic trays – remove and transfer to Tupperware boxes or wrap in greaseproof paper (not foil). The cheese will keep almost indefinitely in the fridge, but sometimes it will 'weep' a little. Again, this is nothing to worry about.

Slice the cheese if you can, or spoon it if it's a bit on the soft and sticky side. Serve with good bread, good cheese (the other kind) and good wine.

Variation: **Damson cheese**
This is another great cheese – arguably every bit as good as quince. Because of the higher liquid content in the damsons it's made in a slightly different way.

Cook **2 kilos of damsons** with just a couple of tablespoons of water, simmering gently until completely soft and tender. Rub through a sieve to remove the stones and skin and give a smooth purée. Measure the purée by volume and add **350g sugar for every 500ml**.

Place in a heavy-based pan and bring to a simmer over a low heat, stirring to dissolve the sugar. Then cook as for quince cheese, above, to a thick, grainy paste.

The high pectin content means that this is a more reliable setter than the quince, so the oven treatment is not necessary. I simply pour this cheese into shallow Tupperware containers and leave to cool. It keeps almost indefinitely in the fridge. Serve in the same way.

feb   mar   apr   may   jun   jul   aug   sep   oct   nov   dec

NOVEMBER_____

For me, November is a meat month. This is not so much because vegetables are in decline – the sun-loving summer crops may be over, but many fine things, such as kale, cabbages, leeks and roots, are at their sweetest and best right now. It's partly because my boat usually comes out of the water at the beginning of the month, for a rest-up and a bit of winter maintenance. It's a poignant moment – a reluctant acknowledgement that the long, carefree days of summer are gone for another half-year. It's frustrating, too, because there's still good fishing to be had. Prawns and sea bass in particular can all be taken at their best this month.

The one winter I tried to flout the local seasonal wisdom and kept *Sea Fox* in the harbour for the winter, the weather unambiguously made its point. I managed a single trip mid-November, in which I barely succeeded in baiting and throwing my pots before a gale blew up. I was forced back into port before I could get a lure in the water for the monster bass I'd felt sure I was destined to catch. And I never saw those pots again.

It was a salutary lesson. Certain man-made 'seasons' may seem arbitrary, and the West Bay boating season (May Bank Holiday to Bonfire Night) undoubtedly falls into that category. But when such a tradition is born of generations of experience, you ignore it at your peril.

However, what really make this month meaty are pork and game (sometimes in joyous combination, as on page 222). We always kill our remaining pair of pigs in November. Then we set about creating our winter supply of bacon, salami, hams, sausages and other charcuterie. This all happens, with the help of friends and neighbours and copious quantities of red wine and whisky (though not in the same glass), over one of our 'pig weekends'. It's a hugely satisfying seasonal ritual that marks the transition from the fish- and veg-heavy late-summer months to the carnivorous and comfort-seeking habits of the winter kitchen.

You don't have to rear your own pigs to host a pig weekend. You can buy one, or half of one, from a reliable small producer. Everything you need to know is explained in loving detail in *The River Cottage Cookbook*, so I won't say any more here. I will say more about game, however, as it is clear that the shooting of it is under ever-increasing scrutiny. Those of us who take part in it have no right to complain about that. But we do have a right – I would say a duty – to explain very carefully why we feel entitled to do it.

In the case of shooting, it's perhaps the idea that we find it fun that most upsets our opponents. It's no good denying it. Only an impoverished poacher, of a kind that barely exists in this country today, could claim to shoot for subsistence.

But for me a big part of the pleasure comes from a powerful and unbreakable link between the killing and the eating of what I kill. Shooting a bird, whether you do it with a blowpipe, an arrow or a shotgun, is a test of skill. Succeeding in such an endeavour, whether you are an Amazonian Indian, a peer of the realm or a Dorset smallholder, can give a great feeling of satisfaction. And part of that is because what you have taken has value – as food.

In the case of wild game, such as hare or woodcock, the food value is exceptional. The meat is special, as is the guarantee of quality and welfare: these creatures have eaten a natural diet in a wild environment and flown or roamed free until the moment they are shot. The situation with reared pheasant is more ambiguous. Its infancy is spent as relatively intensively farmed poultry, its adulthood as effectively a wild bird with a feeding station. This makes it fine eating and gives it, on balance, a pretty enviable life compared to that of farmed poultry.

So where game animals are concerned, issues of morality arise not, on the whole, over the way we impinge on their life but the manner in which we bring about their death – with guns, for our amusement. To the moral vegetarian, this is never likely to be acceptable. But to those who do eat meat, I would say, surely the taking of wild creatures, with guns, is at least preferable to the systematic incarceration of domestic stock in factory farming. Which is to say, an element of inefficiency in the slaughter is offset by the (almost) complete freedom of the creatures during their lifetime. And, for the utilitarian at least, the fact that we enjoy the process should add to rather than detract from its moral acceptability.

It's an argument that's inextricably linked with the food value of game. But these days, sadly, not all birds shot for sport are destined for the pot. The problem is that shooting is not just a countryman's hobby, it's big business. It's a business, landowners will say in their defence, that allows them to manage their land to a conservation agenda, maintaining woodlands and hedgerows for the benefit of many wild native species, as well as for their captive reared game birds. And it's a business that provides a top-quality food product – healthy and free range, if not exactly wild – that many are happy to pay for.

I find this a reasonably robust argument. But there is a point at which it suddenly and dramatically collapses. In recent seasons, pheasants have been raised and shot in such vast numbers that no market could be found to take them all. Consequently birds have been buried in mass graves or simply ploughed into the fields. Such massacres of apparently disposable birds put any possibility of a convincing moral defence under the greatest possible strain.

In my opinion, much of the problem lies in the simplistic way in which most shoots that are run as businesses charge their clients for a day's sport. With few exceptions, the price paid is per bird (from £10–25, depending on where you are in the country). A 'client host' or syndicate tells the landowner or shoot manager how many birds they would like to shoot in a day, and the gamekeeper and his team of beaters do their best to oblige.

Personally I have always found it odd and, in a curiously literal way, unsavoury that the pleasure you get from a day's shooting (and therefore the price you are prepared to pay for it) should be so directly correlated to the number of birds you shoot. What about the landscape, the exercise, and the abundant wildlife you will see at which you do not point your gun? I fear also that the pay-per-bird system undermines the vital connection between the sport of shooting and the pleasures of eating game.

Where I shoot in Dorset, with a couple of local farmers and a few friends, we'd be lucky to fire ten shots each in a day. The last time we went out, the bag was fourteen pheasants, four pigeons, three woodcock, one snipe and a squirrel. For that bag, six guns and a similar number of beaters and dogs worked hard up the hedges, through the woods and across the fields, from nine in the morning until three in the afternoon. When we finally stopped for lunch, I was so hungry that I was tempted by the thought of pheasant sushi. As it was, an enormous beef stew with dumplings did the refuelling job – with admirable lack of restraint all round. And when we were done, we parted, with a couple of birds each, to contemplate the considerable pleasures of the day and the further feast to come. It was a good feeling.

Pear, apple and beetroot salad

Autumn and winter cooking isn't *just* about indulgence and stodge. It's important that you counter the comfort food from time to time with dishes that are fresh and zesty. This unusual salad is a good example. You could eat it as a starter, or as a 'dessert salad' after something simple like soup or cheese on toast.

To serve 4

For each diner, take **1 crisp apple** such as Cox's or Russet, **1 firm but not quite ripe pear** and **1 medium-sized raw beetroot**. Peel them all. Now you can either grate them coarsely, chop them finely, or shred them on the 'matchstick' setting of one of those plastic mandoline slicing gadgets. Discard the cores of the apple and pear when you get to them.

Dress with a good squeeze of **lemon juice** and a trickle of **olive oil**. Season with **salt** and **pepper**. Toss everything together and serve. The salad doesn't keep well (after a few hours the pear and apple will start to discolour), so eat it all up!

Scallops with spiced sausage meat

The combination of pork with shellfish is a proven delight, especially in the cooking of Portugal. Sweet scallops love a bit of spice, and this combination works a treat. You could use spicy frying chorizo from a good deli, but it's great fun to make your own.

To serve 4

Rinse, trim and pat dry **12–16 fresh scallops**, depending on size. Leave the corals on if they are fat and bright orange, but discard them if they are grey-brown and withered. If the scallops are very large, slice them horizontally through the middle, turning 1 scallop into 2 scallop escalopes, if you get my drift. If keeping the corals, then cut so as to leave the whole coral on one half of the scallop.

feb   mar   apr   may   jun   jul   aug   sep   oct   nov   dec

Mix **250g good-quality sausage meat** with 2–3 finely chopped **cloves of garlic**, 1 heaped teaspoon **sweet paprika** and the same of **smoked paprika** (if you can get it), 1 teaspoon **fennel seeds**, up to ½ teaspoon **cayenne pepper**, a pinch of **salt** and freshly ground **black pepper**. Leave in the fridge for at least an hour or, better still, overnight.

Form the spiced sausage meat into thumbnail-sized meatballs. Heat a good film of **olive oil** in a large, heavy-based frying pan over a medium heat. Fry the meatballs, not too fast, shaking the pan occasionally, until well cooked and lightly crispy. Remove with a spatula and keep in a warmed dish. Turn up the heat, so the oil in the pan is almost smoking. Add the scallops at once, turn them after a minute, and cook for no more than 2 minutes overall. Remove the pan from the heat and add the meatballs again, shaking them up to combine with the scallops. Serve without delay, either plain or over a bed of undressed rocket leaves.

French onion tart

This is an absolute classic, which I have been cooking for years. It seems to come into its own around autumn, although it's good at any time of year. It makes a great standby dish, as the ingredients often seem to be knocking about in the kitchen, but I'd happily serve it to honoured guests, too. My version is based on Elizabeth David's recipe in *French Provincial Cooking*, and the only liberty I have taken is to add a little grated Gruyère.

To serve 6

Make some **savoury shortcrust pastry**, line a 20–23cm loose-bottomed tart tin with it, then line with greaseproof paper, add baking beans and bake blind for about 10 minutes.

If you need help with that, the easiest pastry recipe I know is also Elizabeth David's: rub **100g butter** into **200g plain flour** and a pinch of **salt**. Add just enough cold water to bring the mixture together and press it straight into a tart tin, using your hands and fingertips, without even rolling or chilling. Line with greaseproof paper, fill with clay baking beans (or actual dried beans) and cook for about 15 minutes at 200°C/Gas Mark 6. Then remove the paper and beans and return the pastry case to the oven for 5 minutes to dry out the sweaty surface. The resulting pastry is superbly short, crumbly and delicious.

Peel and very finely slice **a kilo of onions**. Heat **50g butter** and 1 tablespoon **olive or sunflower oil** in a large pan and add the onions. Cook very gently, tossing or stirring regularly, without allowing the onions to catch on the pan or turn brown. After about half an hour they should be golden and completely tender. Remove from the heat and season with a pinch of **salt**, a little grated **nutmeg** and a few twists of **black pepper**.

With a fork, beat together **3 egg yolks** and **200ml double cream**. Finely grate about **100g Gruyère cheese**. In the pan, if you like, or in a mixing bowl, combine the onions with the cheese and the egg and cream mixture. Spread evenly into the pre-baked pastry case and put into a fairly hot oven (190°C/Gas Mark 5) for about half an hour, until the filling is lightly puffed and golden. Serve piping hot from the oven.

Variation: Leek and bacon tart

Use **a kilo of leeks**, thoroughly washed and finely shredded, instead of the onions, and sprinkle the base of the pastry case with about **125g lightly fried, roughly chopped bacon or pancetta** before adding the filling as above.

- -

Richard's parsnip risotto

This is a recipe from my editor, Richard Atkinson, who told me it was a winter staple and a great favourite. I'm glad he insisted I try it. It's a lovely dish. I don't think the Italians are very familiar with the parsnip but they would probably acknowledge and approve of the similarity, deriving from the natural sweetness of the parsnip, between this dish and their classic pumpkin risotto. It turns out that the combination of parsnips and generous quantities of Parmesan, about which I was initially sceptical, works extremely well.

feb   mar   apr   may   jun   jul   aug   sep   oct   nov   dec

To serve 2 as a main course, 4 as a starter

Peel **a couple of large parsnips** and chop them into 1cm dice, cutting out and discarding the woody core. Chop **an onion** and cook with a generous slice of **butter** in a heavy-based pan over a medium heat. After 2–3 minutes, when the onion is becoming translucent, add the parsnips, raise the heat a little and cook until almost completely tender, stirring frequently to prevent sticking. Meanwhile, bring about **900ml chicken or vegetable stock** to simmering point in a separate pan.

When the parsnip pieces are soft, add **175g Arborio rice** and stir constantly for a couple of minutes. If you like, and there's a bottle open, add a decent slosh of **white wine** and continue to stir until it has been absorbed by the rice. Then start to ladle hot stock into the risotto, waiting for each batch of stock to be absorbed before adding the next. Keep stirring and adding stock till the rice is tender, with just the tiniest residual chalky 'bite' in the middle. Taste and adjust the seasoning. Stir in a good handful of freshly grated **Parmesan** and serve with plenty of freshly ground **black pepper** and more grated Parmesan on the table.

- -

Roast partridge and all the trimmings

As partridges become more and more popular with British sportsmen and women, so they are becoming more readily available, and cheaper. It's a delicately flavoured and delicious game bird, which often appeals to those who don't like strong-tasting game.

For each person

You need **1 whole partridge**, plucked and drawn, the **neck** and **giblets** reserved. There's not much meat on the wings of a partridge, so I like to clip them off with poultry shears and add them to the stock for the gravy. Ideally you should make this stock in advance.

Roast or fry the necks, wings and giblets from the birds in a little **oil** for 10 minutes, until nicely browned. Roughly chop them up and put them in a small pan with a **bay leaf,**

a chopped **carrot**, a sliced **onion**, ½ **glass of wine** and enough water to cover by a good 5cm. Bring to the boil and simmer gently for an hour or two, topping up if necessary. Then strain – first through a colander, then through cotton or muslin into a clean pan. Boil until reduced by about half, so you have a cup or so of well-flavoured stock for your gravy. (If this sounds laborious you can skip it, but it does help make better gravy, and more of it.)

Make bread sauce by roughly tearing up **100g stale white bread** and putting it in a pan with **250ml whole milk**. Add **a small onion**, peeled, cut in half and studded with a couple of **cloves**, and a few twists of **black pepper**. Leave to soak for an hour or so, then add a knob of **butter** and heat very gently, stirring regularly, adding a little more milk if it gets too thick. Allow to bubble for just a couple of minutes, then remove from the heat and keep warm. Check and adjust the seasoning. Remove and discard the clove-studded onion before serving.

Prepare the birds by smearing a little soft **butter or olive oil** over the breasts and covering each one with **2 streaky bacon rashers**. Place in a roasting tin and put in the centre of a very hot oven (230°C/Gas Mark 8). Remove the bacon from the birds after 8–10 minutes and take it out of the oven if it's as crisp as you'd like it to be. At this point you could baste the birds with any fat in the tin, but do it fast, so as not to let the oven cool. About 15 minutes in total should be enough to cook a small partridge through without drying it, 20 minutes for a larger bird. In both cases rest for 10–15 minutes while you prepare the gravy.

Now make the gravy. Skim off any excess fat from the roasting tin. Sprinkle just a teaspoon of **flour** over the juices in the tin and scrape over the base with a spatula, scratching up any crispy bits and mixing them with the flour and juices. Use a small splash of **wine** and a little of the reserved stock to loosen the gravy. Now strain all the liquid through a sieve into a small saucepan. Whisk in the rest of the stock and bring to the boil. Taste the gravy, adding a little **redcurrant jelly** if you think it needs sweetness. Boil to reduce it if you want to intensify the flavour. In short, fix the gravy how you like it.

I don't generally carve partridges but serve a whole small bird or half a large one per person, to be tackled on the plate – fingers allowed. Serve each bird with its bacon and a handful of game chips (good-quality potato crisps, heated in the oven, are fine). Bring the piping-hot gravy, bread sauce and either buttered steamed greens (such as curly kale or Savoy cabbage) or a salad of watercress, rocket or other winter greens to the table. Tuck in.

Pikelets

When it's cold outside and dark by late afternoon, the occasional baking of teatime treats is one of the great pleasures and comforts of the kitchen. And there are few greater treats than hot buttered crumpets. As a child I always assumed that some special tool – resembling a round, stout-bristled hairbrush, perhaps – was needed to make the holes in the crumpets. In fact, the holes appear as the raising agent does its thing while they cook on the griddle plate.

The recipe I'm going to give is for a slight variation on the theme: pikelets are similar in texture to crumpets but a little less hassle, as they can be cooked without a crumpet ring. They'll end up thinner than a crumpet, but they'll still have those lovely holes to soak up the melting butter. They keep well, and can be stored in a sealed plastic bag or box in the fridge for 2–3 days. They freeze well too. Reheat on a griddle or in a toaster before serving.

To make about 30

Sift **250g strong white bread flour, 250g plain flour**, ¾ teaspoon **cream of tartar** and 1 teaspoon **salt** into a large mixing bowl. Crumble **15g fresh yeast** into a small bowl. Cream it to a smooth paste with a little lukewarm water, then stir in more until you've added 500ml warm water altogether (or use dried or Easyblend yeast, according to the instructions on the packet, adding enough for 500g flour). Pour the yeast liquid into the flour to make a very thick, but smooth and glossy batter, beating vigorously with your hand for a couple of minutes. Cover the bowl with a warm, damp cloth and leave to stand in a warm place for up to 2 hours, until the batter is very well risen and frothy.

Dissolve 1 teaspoon **bicarbonate of soda** in **150ml lukewarm whole milk**, then gently stir it into the batter, a little at a time. You may not need all the milk, but the batter should end up the consistency of very thick paint.

Heat a lightly greased flat griddle or heavy frying pan until very hot. Put 1 dessertspoonful at a time of the batter in circles on the griddle. Cook over a medium heat for about 2–3 minutes on each side, turning when the bubbles forming on the surface start to dry out.

Eat hot, straight away, with butter and honey or jam, or sprinkled with sugar and cinnamon. Try a savoury approach, too – those holes are just as generous at receiving trickled olive oil as melted butter, and a rub of garlic, followed by a grating of Parmesan cheese.

feb   mar   apr   may   jun   jul   aug   sep   oct   nov   dec

Bramley burnt creams

This is a pudding my granny used to make and it has always ranked as one of my favourites. The burnt brown sugar gives an irresistible toffee taste, which goes beautifully with the tart apple. It somehow seems perfect to round off a Sunday lunch on a sunny autumn afternoon.

To serve 6 – 8

Peel, core and slice about **a kilo of Bramley apples**, then cook them over a gentle heat with a shake of **caster sugar** and just a dribble of water to prevent them burning. Simmer gently, stirring occasionally, until the apple pieces have completely dissolved. Go on cooking gently and stirring until you have a thick, slightly translucent purée. Add more caster sugar to taste – enough to achieve a purée that is still tart but not unpleasantly so. Leave to cool. Divide the purée between 6–8 ramekins or other small heatproof dishes, leaving a generous centimetre at the top, then chill thoroughly in the fridge.

Whip **330ml double cream** until very thick, then spread it carefully over the chilled apple purée, covering it completely and levelling the cream across the top of the ramekins. Return to the fridge or even, briefly, a freezer, until the cream is thoroughly cold – but not frozen (this chilling allows you to burn the sugar without boiling the cream).

Preheat a grill to maximum. Sprinkle a thin, even layer of **soft brown sugar** over the chilled ramekins (not more than 1 level dessertspoon per ramekin). Place the ramekins under the hot grill until the sugar begins to melt and bubble. The cream underneath may start to bubble up but don't worry if this happens. It may look a bit rough but it will still taste divine. (Those adept with a blowtorch in the kitchen can use this to melt the sugar.)

Return the ramekins to the fridge until they are quite cold. They are then ready to serve – with teaspoons to crack through the hardened sugar to the cream and apple beneath.

DECEMBER_____

In December British cooks can get a bit seasonally jingoistic (or perhaps that should be jingle-istic), as if the festivities at the end of the month were all that mattered. From weeks beforehand (when is Stir Up Sunday? I can never remember), they begin stockpiling seasonal goodies in the larder, to unleash them all in one explosive forty-eight-hour family binge.

I'm anxiously aware that I'm in danger of aiding and abetting this Christmas culinary fever in this chapter. Because, after much reflection, I have decided to devote the entire recipe section to the preparation of a single meal – an almighty Christmas family feast, in fact. So before I cut loose and get all festive myself, I want to emphasise a very important point. These recipes, like cute puppies, are not just for Christmas. They are for life during all the colder months. That includes the mince pies. The way I see it, if there is only one day of the year on which a dish gets an outing, it's either because you don't like it or because you are unable to break free from the stifling bonds of tradition. If the former, then why not simply drop it altogether? (Try my chestnut and chocolate truffle cake instead – everybody likes that.) If the latter, then GET A GRIP! Who's in charge here?

To emphasise the point, the picture of my camera-shy wife brandishing a be-Brusselled stem of sprouts (from Washingpool, our charmingly named local farm shop) was scrupulously placed in the January chapter, having been taken in the last week of that month. My sprout dish in this chapter is presented as an accompaniment to the roast goose. But, just as the picture could have been taken in any month between November and March, so my creamed sprouts can be enjoyed at any point during this time frame.

The stretch of availability of the sprout, and much other winter produce, raises an important point about the 'harvest of the cold months', as Elizabeth David so nicely put it. The seasonal transition from autumn to winter is perhaps the least perceptible. The process is effectively one of slowing down until, without ever feeling the bump, any thrust of seasonal change seems to have stopped altogether. My hunch is that this usually happens some time during December, but it's hard to be sure. The effect, however, is dependable: in a culinary, if not a meteorological sense, winter is undoubtedly the longest season.

You might think that this winter torpor would be a limiting factor for the seasonal cook. Whatever things are doing, they are not reaching maturity or getting 'ripe'. A lot of the best fresh produce is surely 'over' – banished from the menu till the following June at the earliest. We may mourn the absence of peas – or run to the freezer to get some. But if we flip the viewpoint we can see what an amazing asset this annual stasis turns out to be. Things do not bloom or fruit. But neither do they bolt or go to seed. What is going to rot has rotted. But what is designed to last may keep now for months.

This includes some of the summer and autumn crops. In cold weather, potatoes and carrots can be stored in cool, dry earth for months. Other roots, such as parsnips, celeriac and salsify, remain stable and sturdy if left in the ground. Onions, shallots and garlic keep all their freshness and potency when in store, till the subtle warmth of March (or the less subtle warmth of a centrally heated kitchen) urges them to sprout their reproductive shoots.

Frost-resistant greens, such as cabbages, kale and Brussels sprouts, will neither grow nor fade. They stay put, the antifreeze in their cellulose doing its job, until the spring sunshine gives them a chance to flower and seed. (If you think about it, it is the eating qualities of the purple sprouting broccoli flowerhead that make it such a brilliant seasonal stopgap. We harvest it at the precise moment its brassica relatives become unpalatable.)

The cook in winter can reap great benefit from this biological inactivity. No longer fretting about courgettes becoming marrows, blackberries turning sour or salads wilting in the first frost, he or she can make a calm appraisal of the things that are built to last. Big questions can be asked, like, 'What's the most exciting thing I can do with an onion?'

From November to February, many of the recipes I offer are intended to provide a variety of answers to this question, not just for onions but for a whole range of winter produce.

feb   mar   apr   may   jun   jul   aug   sep   oct   nov   dec

And many of the recipes apply pretty equally across the four months. So in this chapter, if I appear to be shirking this responsibility in favour of seasonal frivolity, I'm not really. Honest.

Incidentally, I do have an alternative to the goose as the centrepiece of a family Christmas dinner. But it isn't the turkey. I'm afraid he got fired from Christmas dinner several years ago, largely at my instigation. His dismissal from festive duty wasn't a decision we took lightly but, and I think I speak for the whole family here, it certainly isn't one we regret.

It's hard to be precise about why I felt, increasingly, that turkey was failing to deliver. It doesn't have to be bland and dry – though these pitfalls are all too rarely avoided. But even the most organic, best-hung, gamiest, juiciest, crispest-skinned bird – of a kind I feel we achieved at least a couple of times – wasn't doing it for me. Something was missing.

Whether you are religious or not, the Christmas meal is something pretty sacred. It is a time when we are looking to feed our better selves. The food we choose to eat needs to spread love, warmth, goodwill, forgiveness and optimism around a large table of people who, though bonded together by varying levels of shared genes and shared history, might not otherwise choose to sit down and eat together. It needs to weave a spell of magic that suspends any disbelief in the meaning of family, and indeed in the meaning of Christmas. And although normal, sceptical service is likely to resume with the Boxing Day hangover, something of the spirit of that meal should linger deep in the unconscious, helping to keep us sane and sanguine for the next twelve months.

This is a tall order, and the mild, white flesh of turkey, even at its best, simply isn't up to the job. What's required is something heartier, richer and more intense. What's needed is a flesh whose savour runs deep. I said 'sanguine', and on Christmas Day I want to taste blood. Roast goose, served perfectly pink, as in the picture on page 245, is one superb answer to the challenge. And the goose feast described in the pages that follow is now our Christmas dinner every other year.

The alternative, with which we now ring the Christmas changes, is to bring on the beef. Not just any old beef, mind, but a massive, well-aged, beautifully marbled joint of roast forerib on the bone.

But that's another story, and one I'll be saving for my next book, *The River Cottage Meat Book*. With a bit of luck, it should be out just in time for Christmas.

My Christmas goose

This dish, or set of dishes, has become a bit of a signature for me – and a Christmas institution in our house. I love it partly because it is so thrifty and resourceful – a single large goose yields three very different dishes – but mainly because the three dishes in question are all a delight in their own right. They are a salami-style stuffed neck, a confit of the legs, and a traditional roast. Between them they express all the versatility of this wonderful bird.

For a celebration meal, such as Christmas dinner, all three dishes can be served in succession, and will be enough for six people. The full final menu, in all its formal glory (you'll have to imagine sprigs of holly and glittering golden bells decorating the script, because Georgia, my designer, wouldn't let me have them), is as follows:

Giblet-stuffed neck of goose
with winter leaves and spicy chutney

Confit of goose legs with
split pea and peppercorn purée

Roast goose with roast winter vegetables,
creamed sprouts, apple sauce and all the trimmings

Or, for a more thrifty approach, the confit of legs can be preserved for months, covered with goose fat. If you are rearing your own geese, it makes sense to kill several at once and make a batch of the confit and neck sausage. The remaining 'breast joint' freezes well.

To prepare my goose properly takes a little time, and if you plan to eat all three dishes together you should begin at least three days before the meal. But it's a gleeful task in which several willing hands can all do their bit. The final, huge advantage is that relatively little labour is required on the day itself, leaving the head chef plenty of time to enjoy the meal, not to mention the plaudits of family and friends.

General instructions follow to help you plan this as a single celebration meal. After that, I'll deal with all the recipes, including the various accompaniments, one by one.

Ordering the goose

If you are not providing the goose yourself it is vital that you specify how you want the bird: an ordinary oven-ready goose is not ideal, as certain vital bits (such as the skin of the neck) will be missing. So either contact the best butcher you know and explain what it is you are after or, better still, do a bit of research and buy a goose direct from the producer.

What you need is a whole large goose, preferably organic or free range. The neck and all the giblets are essential for the neck sausage, and you may as well take the feet for stock, if they are going. If you are anxious about cutting up the bird yourself, then by all means get your butcher to take the legs off it and cut off the neck, but explain what you are planning to do, so that he or she prepares everything just as you need it. In particular, explain that you are planning to stuff the goose's neck, so it needs to be cut off as close as possible to the head and breast, and the skin must be left on – it is going to be the casing of a giant sausage.

Stuffing the neck isn't as difficult a procedure as you might think, and there is every chance of first-time success if you carefully follow the instructions below. But if it all sounds too much like a palaver, or if you can't get hold of a whole bird with the neck intact but still have the giblets, then this recipe can easily be adapted to make a terrine, which can be made in a suitable dish and cooked in the oven in a *bain-marie* in the usual way. Instructions for this variation are given in the recipe on page 243.

Preparing the goose for the three dishes

Collect your goose three to five days before your planned meal (i.e. from the 20th to 22nd December for Christmas Day). First remove the excess fat (there should be plenty) from inside the cavity of the bird. This fat is essential for cooking both the confit and the stuffed neck.

Now cut off the legs – not just the drumstick but the thigh bone too, and the lovely scallop of meat that attaches to it. To do this, cut through the skin where the leg joins the body, then push the whole leg away from the breast. This will expose the ball and socket joint where the thighbone joins the body of the goose. Don't be afraid to push hard enough to tear the ligaments around this joint. Then use the knife to cut through the tough sinews. With the thigh, cut away that scallop of meat I mentioned by following the natural contours of the muscle meat that attaches to the thigh, being careful not to impinge on the lower part of

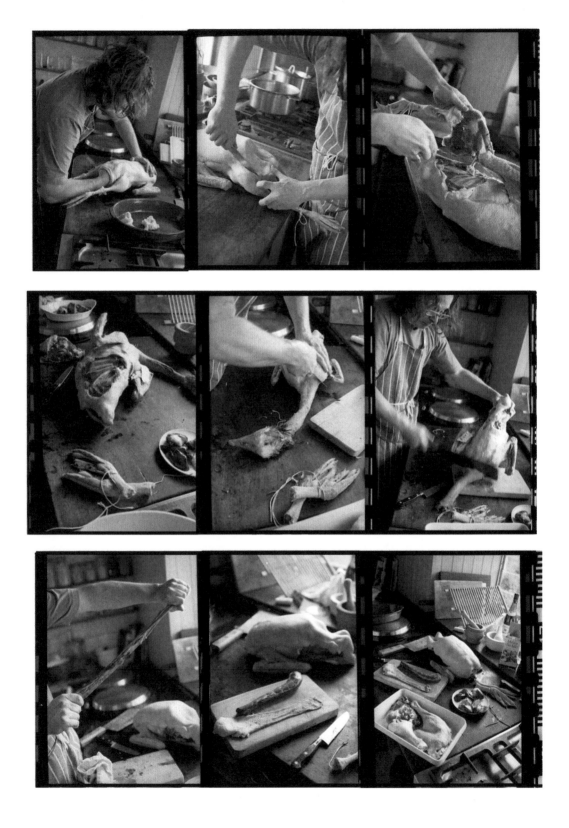

the breast muscle on the bird. Cut off the feet, below the drumstick joint. The first few pictures of the sequence opposite will help you to understand exactly how all this is done.

Then remove the neck: using the point of a very sharp knife, cut around the skin at the base of the neck, incorporating a good-sized flap of skin all round from the part where the neck joins the body. Once you have released the skin, you can cut through the neck muscle and bones with a cleaver or poultry shears – again, as near the base as possible. If the head is still attached at the other end of the neck, cut it off. Peel off the skin from the neck, carefully and in one piece – remember it's your sausage casing. Remove and discard the windpipe. Remove any excess fat inside the skin of the neck and put it with the rest of the fat to be rendered.

You are now left with a legless, neckless carcass of goose, which is more or less oven-ready. Cover it with a cloth and return it to the fridge, or a very cool larder, until you want to roast it. The head and feet are the only parts of the bird that you may throw away, though even they could go in the stockpot.

The fat must now be rendered: put all the fat, and fatty pieces, in an ovenproof dish and into a moderate oven (180°C/Gas Mark 4). After half an hour, strain all the melted fat through a sieve into a bowl. Return the dish to the oven and repeat the straining every 15 minutes or so, until all the fat has been rendered. Leave the rendered fat to cool, and keep it in the bowl until you need it.

Now you're ready to tackle the three recipes, as follows . . .

- -

Confit of goose legs

Confit means 'preserved' in French, as in the word *confiture*, meaning jam. In the goose-producing regions of France, such as Gascony and Cahors, preserving part of the annual harvest used to be a way of extending the shelf life of the goose through the winter months. In that respect, confit is the poultry equivalent of bacon and hams.

feb   mar   apr   may   jun   jul   aug   sep   oct   nov   dec

Salt the legs at least 48 hours before you plan to serve the dish. The first long cooking can be done the day before your meal, and the final crisping up just before serving.

Crush together into a paste **25g flaky salt**, a good teaspoon of freshly ground **black pepper**, the stripped, chopped leaves from several sprigs of **thyme**, a couple of shredded **bay leaves** and **3 large cloves of garlic**. Rub this mixture thoroughly into the skin and meat of your goose legs. Leave for 48 hours in a tray or dish in the fridge, giving the legs another salty massage after 24 hours. Then scrape off all these seasonings and reserve.

Heat a film of **goose fat or olive oil** in a heavy pan over a moderate heat and brown the legs thoroughly in it, skin-side down first and then all over. Put the legs into an ovenproof dish in which they fit as snugly as possible, with the seasoning scrapings and enough **rendered goose fat or lard** to cover, or almost cover, the meat. Then cook for at least 3 hours in a very slow oven (120°C/Gas Mark ½), until the meat is nearly falling from the bone. If the legs are not quite covered by the fat, turn them carefully 2 or 3 times during cooking.

Remove from the oven and leave to cool. To preserve the confit legs, put them into a large Kilner jar or similar, or into a plastic tub with a lid, and pour over enough warm liquid goose fat or lard to cover completely and seal the meat from the air. Leave until they are cold and the fat is set hard, then cover with the lid. Thus preserved, the confit will keep for several months in a cool larder or even longer in the fridge. Or simply smeared in fat and wrapped in clingfilm, it will still keep for a good couple of weeks in the fridge.

When the confit is to be served, remove the legs from the container and scrape off most (not all) of the fat – rendered and filtered, it can be used again. Place the legs skin-side down in a roasting tin. Put into a hot oven (230°C/Gas Mark 8) for 5 minutes, drain off the melted fat, then return to the oven for 5–10 minutes, skin-side up, until crisp and piping hot.

Traditionally a confit like this is served on the bone, one leg per (very hungry) person, accompanied by beans or lentils. But for my special Christmas menu it's served, as in the last frame opposite, with the split pea and peppercorn purée on page 240. As part of such a feast, each guest only needs a taster. So shred all the meat and skin off the bones, like Chinese waiters do with crispy duck. Spoon a pool of the hot purée into the middle of a hot plate, and a pile of shredded confit on top of that. Serve with **orange slices** either on the plates or on the table, as palate-refreshers to cut the fat of the goose.

Split pea and peppercorn purée

This dish, an old favourite, is particularly recommended as an accompaniment to the confit of goose legs in the Christmas menu. The whole peppercorns make little punchy explosions in contrast to the smooth, slightly sweetish purée and the rich, fatty meat. But it also goes very nicely with roast lamb and any roast game birds. Bulked out with a few chunks of bacon or ham, it makes a good wintry supper dish on its own.

To serve 6 as an accompaniment to the confit, 2 as a supper dish

Soak **250g split peas** overnight in plenty of cold water, if you have time. Drain, rinse and put into a saucepan with a **bay leaf** and a few stock vegetables, such as **a small onion**, peeled and halved, **a large carrot**, peeled and cut into chunks, and **a stick or two of celery**, cut into chunks. Add just enough water to cover them. Bring to the boil and simmer gently until tender. If the peas are beginning to boil dry, add a little boiling water.

When the peas are completely soft, you should be able to mash them into a rough purée with a potato masher – or even by beating with a wooden spoon. But you can use a food processor, if you like. Remove from the heat, discard the vegetables and bay leaf, then beat, mash or process the peas with a good knob of **butter** and season to taste with **salt** and a pinch of **sugar**. Add 1 tablespoon **green or pink peppercorns pickled in brine** and mix well in.

Heat through before serving, thinning with a little hot water if the purée is very stiff.

- -

Giblet-stuffed neck of goose

The neck can be stuffed and cooked any time on the days preceding Christmas. You can even cook it with the confit if you like. If you do the terrine version, it is best made a day or two before. I usually serve the neck cold, as the first of the three courses, but recently I tried it hot, served with the confit as one of only two courses, and I liked it a lot. Take your pick.

Place the neck skin in a small dish, cover with a couple of tablespoons of **brandy or rum** and leave to marinate until you are ready to stuff it. This helps to soften the skin, so that it will stretch when stuffed and not split.

Chop the skinless neck into a few sections and put in a pan with the **heart** and **gizzard**, a few **stock vegetables** and a **bay leaf** (you can also include the **feet** of the bird, scrubbed clean, and the **head**, skinned, if you have kept them). Cover with cold water, bring to the boil and simmer gently for 1½–2 hours. Strain the stock and put aside – you'll use it to make the gravy for the roast goose (page 244). Discard the vegetables, and the feet and head if used, and leave the heart, gizzard and neck pieces to cool.

Pick off as much meat as you can from the neck. Trim the coarse edges off the gizzard. Roughly chop the neck meat, gizzard and heart and put in a mixing bowl. Finely chop the fresh **liver** of the bird and add to the bowl. Add **125g good sausage meat**, a nugget of **rendered goose fat or butter**, a few sprigs of fresh **thyme** and/or 6–10 fresh **sage leaves**, both finely chopped, a few scrapes of **nutmeg**, 1 tablespoon of the brandy or rum marinade and another of **port**. Season well with **salt** and **black pepper**. Mix all these ingredients thoroughly with your hands, until well combined.

Now it's time to stuff the neck skin. There are two effective ways to seal each end of it. The easiest is simply to tie each end tightly with several turns of butcher's string and a few reef knots. Tie the narrow head end first, then stuff in as much of the forcemeat as you can (be gentle but firm and the skin should stretch to accommodate a surprising amount of stuffing; don't overstretch it, though, or it may split when cooking). Then tie the other end in the same way.

The more skilful way, which allows you to get a bit more stuffing in the neck, is to use a darning needle and extra-strong cotton to sew up each end. I can't really give precise guidance on the stitching technique but I think it's what my mother calls blanket stitch. If you fancy your needlework skills you'll probably make a better job of it than I do.

The stuffed neck is gently simmered in hot **goose fat** – topped up with **lard** if necessary. This can be done in a large pan on the hob, over a low heat, or in a deep roasting tin in a slow oven (about 120°C/Gas Mark ½). Either way, the sausage should be pricked in several places with a needle to ensure it doesn't burst. Then lower it carefully into the

preheated fat so it is covered, or almost covered. If it's not completely covered you should turn it every 10 minutes or so.

You can, if it suits you, cook the stuffed neck in the same dish as the confit during its initial slow cooking (having kept the neck, stuffed but uncooked, in the fridge for a day or two if you're waiting for the confit to cure). It won't take as long as the confit, though – about 1¼ hours should do it.

The stuffed neck can now be served hot, with the confit if you like, accompanied by beans, lentils or my special split pea purée (page 240). Or, once cooked, remove it from the fat, leave to cool completely, wrap in foil and refrigerate. It can be kept for a couple of days and, like a pâté or terrine, the flavour will improve.

Then, to serve it up cold as a course on its own, remove from the fridge and foil about an hour before dinner. Slice thickly and serve each guest a couple of slices, on a plate dressed with a few **winter salad leaves**, with a blob of **spicy, fruity chutney** on the side.

Variation: **The terrine version**

If you have been unable to get a bird with the neck skin on, but have still managed to procure the giblets, this makes an easy alternative to the stuffed neck.

Make the stuffing exactly as above, but add to it 1 tablespoon **breadcrumbs** and **an egg**. Line a small loaf tin or ceramic terrine dish with **streaky bacon rashers**, stretched with the back of a knife, and pile in the mixture. Cover with a lid or a double layer of foil and bake in a tray of hot water in a moderate oven (170°C/Gas Mark 3) for 1½ hours. Remove and leave to cool a little. Cut a piece of thick card or thin wood to fit neatly inside the tin, and wrap it with foil. Place on top of the terrine and weight down with weights, jars or stones. Leave to cool completely.

Serve a single thick slice of terrine per person, garnished with leaves and accompanied by chutney, as with the neck.

Roast goose with roast winter vegetables, apple sauce and gravy

The first two courses show a distinctly French approach to the extraneous parts of the goose. I like to give the main body of the bird a more traditionally British treatment.

Prick the surface of the breast all over with a sharp fork and rub well with a little rough **salt** and **pepper**. It can be served ever so slightly pink, which is best achieved by roasting fast in a hot oven (220°C/Gas Mark 7) for about 50 minutes. Let it rest for 20 minutes before carving. Here's how to fix the accompaniments:

The gravy

The basis for your gravy is the **stock** in which the giblets, neck (and maybe the feet and head) of the goose were cooked. After the initial cooking, this stock should be strained and refrigerated, so the fat, which will set on the top, can then easily be removed. Then warm up the stock and strain it through a cloth or muslin into a clean, heavy-based pan. Add one third as much **red wine** as there is stock and bring to the boil to reduce. The stronger the reduction, the less you need for each guest. I like to think in terms of a tablespoon per person of pretty strong stuff, and so I reduce it to about 200ml. Do not season with salt or pepper until the end or it will become unpalatably salty (and peppery) as it reduces. If you like a thicker gravy, whisk a little *beurre manié* (soft butter mixed to a paste with plain flour) into the boiling juices until you get the thickness you require.

The gravy can be supplemented at the last moment by the juices strained from the roasting tin, deglazed with another splash of red wine. But skim off as much fat as you can and whisk the gravy well to incorporate the little that inevitably gets through.

The apple sauce

Peel, core and slice **3 large Bramleys** and cook them with just a tablespoon of water, a small knob of **butter** and 1 tablespoon **caster sugar** until they disintegrate. Keep simmering gently for 10 minutes or so until you have a nice, thick apple purée. Sweeten to taste with a little more caster sugar if you like (I recommend you keep it tart to cut the fat of the goose).

Serving up the roast

I like to carve the roast at (or beside) the table, in the traditional manner. With two courses already dispatched, a couple of thin slices of breast per person, plus at least one piece each of the various different roast vegetables (see opposite), a good trickle of the very rich gravy, a 'quenelle' of creamed sprouts (see below) and a generous tablespoon of the apple sauce, should keep everybody happy.

Creamed sprouts with bacon

Some people think they don't like sprouts. Try this simple and delicious concoction on them and ask them to think again. It works as a great accompaniment to the Christmas roast, be it goose or turkey or a hot, glazed Christmas ham. But it's also a nice supper dish on its own.

To serve 6 as a side dish, 2 for supper

Roast about **250g chestnuts** in advance: make a small slit in each one to prevent explosions, then toast them on a shovel in the fire, or in a dry heavy frying pan on the hob, turning frequently, until nicely charred and cooked through. This takes about 10–15 minutes. Peel when cool enough to handle, removing the thin, brown inner skin too. Then roughly chop or crumble them.

Trim **500g Brussels sprouts** and simmer gently in well-salted water for 8–10 minutes, until just tender. Drain, put in a food processor with a knob of **butter** and 2 tablespoons **double cream** and pulse several times until you have a rough, creamy purée.

Cut up **4–6 thick streaky bacon rashers** into 5 or 6 pieces each and fry them until crisp. Stir the chestnut pieces into the creamed sprouts and gently heat through until thoroughly hot. Spread into a warmed dish and sprinkle over the crispy bacon bits. Serve at once.

Roast winter vegetables

While this is an essential and luxurious accompaniment to the roast goose in my trio of goose dishes above, it also constitutes a wonderful dish in its own right. Goose fat, if carefully used, can be recycled several times, and a dish of vegetables roasted in goose fat is easily delicious enough to get a solo outing as a supper dish once in a while.

Any of the following vegetables can be roasted in a good 1cm depth of **rendered goose fat**. (Truth be told, good-quality lard, beef dripping or best olive oil can also be used to delicious effect.) The fat or oil should be thoroughly heated in a roasting tin in a fairly hot oven (200°C/Gas Mark 6) before any of the vegetables go in. They do not all take the same time to cook, so can be added at staggered intervals. All should be turned once or twice during cooking and seasoned towards the end with **salt** and **pepper**.

To serve up, drain the roasted vegetables on kitchen paper, pile them in a hot dish, give a generous final seasoning of salt and pepper, and take to the table.

Basic preparation and cooking times are given below:

Potatoes – peeled, par-boiled for 5 minutes in well-salted water, cut as you like, and scratched with a fork: 40–45 minutes.

Parsnips – peeled and cut as you like: 30–35 minutes.

Celeriac – peeled and cut into 5cm cubes: 30–35 minutes.

Jerusalem artichokes – scrubbed and dried, but unpeeled and left whole: 30–35 minutes.

Swede – peeled and cut into large chunks: 30–35 minutes.

Beetroot – raw, peeled and cut into large chunks: 30–35 minutes.

Pumpkins and squashes – in chunks, seeds removed but unpeeled: 30 minutes.

Carrots – big donkey carrots, peeled and cut into large chunks: 30 minutes.

Shallots (or baby onions) – whole and in their skins: 30 minutes.

Garlic – whole bulbs in their skins: 30 minutes.

Leeks – cut into 5cm lengths: 20 minutes.

- -

feb   mar   apr   may   jun   jul   aug   sep   oct   nov   dec

Chestnut and chocolate cake

This is a really wonderful soft and gooey chocolate cake, which can be served warm or cold as a pudding. It makes a great alternative for anyone who's not so keen on traditional Christmas pudding – and it's also an absolute doddle to make.

To serve 8 – 10

Melt **250g dark chocolate** and **250g unsalted butter** together in a pan over a very gentle heat. In another pan, heat **250g peeled cooked chestnuts** (tinned if you like) with **250ml milk** until just boiling, then mash thoroughly with a potato masher (or process to a rough purée in a machine).

Separate **4 eggs**, put the yolks in a bowl and mix with **125g caster sugar**. Stir in the chocolate mixture and the chestnut purée until you have a smooth, blended batter. Whisk the egg whites until stiff and fold them carefully into the batter. Transfer the mixture to a greased, lined 25cm cake tin (the springform type is good) and bake at 170°C/Gas Mark 3 for 25–30 minutes, until it is just set but still has a slight wobble.

If you want to serve the cake warm, leave to cool a little, then release the tin and slice carefully – it will be very soft and moussey. Or leave to go cold, when it will have set firm. I like to serve it with a trickle of double cream, especially when warm, but it is also delicious unadulterated.

- -

Real meat mince pies

This is a recipe from the good old days, when mincemeat was what it said it was – a highly spiced condiment containing meat. This makes some people squeamish, but really there is nothing to fear. The meat is 'invisible'. But its inclusion means that mince pies made from this mincemeat are less sweet and sickly than the usual fare, and have more body and substance. I guarantee you will love them.

jan   feb   mar   apr   may   jun   jul   aug   sep   oct   nov   dec

The quality of the beef is important: it should be lean and free from tough sinews. I like to buy braising or chuck steak and trim and mince it myself. Make the mincemeat at least a week, ideally a month, before you use it. It also makes a great stuffing for a loin of pork.

To make 5–6 jam jars of mincemeat

500g finely minced lean beef
250g beef suet
250g currants
250g raisins
500g tart eating apples, peeled, cored and finely chopped
200g soft brown sugar
125g ground almonds
100g preserved ginger in syrup, finely chopped, plus 4 tablespoons **syrup** from the jar
100g mixed candied peel, finely chopped
grated zest and juice of **1 lemon**
grated zest and juice of **1 orange**
½ teaspoon freshly grated **nutmeg**
2 teaspoons **ground mixed spice**
250ml rum, brandy or Calvados

Put everything in a large bowl and mix thoroughly, ideally with your hands. Keep in sealed jars in a cool place for up to a month before using. Make into mince pies using your favourite sweet pastry recipe, or a bought pastry. As you can see, I favour a very simple folded-over crescent shape, which requires no messing about with pastry lids or moulded tins. Just use a little water or egg wash to seal the edges. Bake at 180°C/Gas Mark 4 for 15–20 minutes, until golden brown.

Serve piping hot with either brandy butter or a rich egg custard laced with Calvados, rum or brandy. Merry Christmas, everybody – and indeed, HAPPY NEW YEAR!